H. R. MEHTA

A HISTORY OF THE GROWTH AND DEVELOPMENT OF WESTERN EDUCATION IN THE PUNJAB

1846—1884

Nirmal Publishers & Distributors
B-2, VISHAL ENCLAVE, NEW DELHI-110027

Published by
NIRMAL PUBLISHERS AND DISTRIBUTORS
B-2, Vishal Enclave, New Delhi-110027
Phone : 5413460

Reprint : 1987

Price : Rs. 50-00

Printed at
Anubhav Art Press
Raghubir Nagar, New Delhi-110027

PREFATORY NOTE.

In the following monograph Mr. Mehta gives in detail the story of the development of Western Education in the Punjab. The problems which faced the British in 1849 were many and varied. There was the question of the retention of the existing system of indigenous education—of which the author gives a detailed description. There was the question of the medium of instruction under the new condition and of the organization of a proper Education Department and Inspectorate. Then, as the machiney became more complicated, we get to the problems of female and collegiate education. Mr. Mehta has made his story a clear and interesting one and the graphs which illustrate the story of development are of particular value.

Lahore : H. L. O. GARRETT,

September 1929. *Keeper of the Records of Government.*

CONTENTS.

CONTENTS

1

Introduction.

The object of this thesis is to trace the development and progress of education in the Punjab during the 38 years following the Treaty of Lahore when the British first acquired possession of the Punjab soil, *viz.*, the territory between the Beas and the Sutlej, known as the Jullundur Doab and comprising the modern districts of Kangra, Jullundur, and Hoshiarpur or parts thereof. The annexation of the whole province by the British having followed two years later in 1849, the subject of our enquiry practically consists in the efforts of the British Government, from 1846 to 1884, to provide education for the people of the Punjab.

It would be necessary, before we commence the narrative of the educational work of the British, to describe briefly the state of education as it stood in 1846. A knowledge of the material the British had to work upon—its peculiaritics, drawbacks, and possibilities – cannot but be of real value in enabling us to appreciate correctly the efforts they made in this sphere ; the difficulties they encountered, and the measures they adopted to carry the people along with them in the cause of the educational up-lift of the country.

In this thesis, the history of education in the Punjab is divided into two well marked periods. During the first period which extends up to 1854 for about 8 years, the energy of the government was mainly concentrated upon the political settlement of the country and upon the question of providing an efficient machinery to carry on the work of administration. The period under consideration did not therefore allow of its embarking upon any educational experiment of a comprehensive character and, although the subject of popular education was not entirely neglected, yet it was left mostly to the discretion of the Board of Administration to devote what time and attention it could spare from its more pressing duties. To quote from one of the earliest Administration Reports, "Popular education is a matter not easily to be studied and promoted under the pressure of urgent business, which has crowded on the Board ever since annexation. Some initiatory steps have, however, been taken."[1] Therefore, though no all-embracing scheme on education was undertaken, the ground for work was prepared, educational possibilities of the province ascertained as far as possible, and a programme for the future formulated.

We shall then deal with the second period of British Education in the Punjab. It extends over the space of more than a quarter of a century, from 1854 to 1884, or strictly speaking from 1856 to 1884, and is indeed a period of great activity and fruitfulness. It thus occupies the life-period of a full generation and its results and achievements may therefore be adjuged with greater certainty and completeness. The Supreme

[1]Punjab Administration Report 1849-50, paragraph 39.

Government at Calcutta, or rather the Hon'ble Court of Directors at London formulated—by means of their famous Despatch of 1854, re-affirmed by the subsequent despatch of 1859—the main lines of the educational policy to be followed in India. The state was taking up the role, not merely of a guide but also of a controlling agency; the educational system of the whole of India was, in fundamental respects, to be the same; India was to be introduced to Western Culture, and Western methods were to be ingrafted upon the Indian soil. An experiment on so grand a scale fraught with far-reaching consequences to about 270 millions of people is one of the most unique happenings of the world and cannot but be of supreme interest to us. The experiment in the Punjab was carried on by the Education Department under the Provincial Government and what difficulties there were to its working in the Punjab and how far the expected results were achieved, is the aim of the following pages to narrate.

In the concluding year of this period, we shall speak of the work of the Education Commission of 1882, the official body appointed to ascertain the working and results of the experiment in progress during the period and we shall, keeping in view the scope of this book, take note of its chief recommendations concerning the Punjab and the action taken thereon in this province.

Finally, we shall briefly review the achievements of the new system for the spread of education in this province, and consider the effects of education upon the moral and political well-being of the people, so that in the light of the knowledge thus acquired, we might form a clear idea of the needs of the hour and try to devise means to fulfil them.

2

Indigenous Education in the Punjab.

Preliminary remarks.

Education in the Punjab at the advent of the British rule cannot be said to be in a flourishing condition. For more than two centuries before 1849 when it was annexed by the British, the Punjab had hardly known any years of unbroken peace. Being an outlying province of the old sultanate of Delhi,—it indeed formed its north-western frontier—it came to be considered, soon after the decay of the Moghal Empire began, merely as a pawn in the political game and frequently changed hands, passing from the Moghals to the Dauranies and later on given by them to Sikhs or Ranjit Singh. The latter gave the land peace for about thirty years but the Sikh power which rested upon an efficient military organisation contained within itself the germs of its dissolution which became visible as soon as the strong hand of the Sher-i-Punjab had been removed. So it had hardly had any time to consolidate itself and it is therefore not strange that it produced no change in, and left little mark upon, the cultural development of the Punjab. Consequently, it was not the Hindu or Muslim educational systems or institutions in their palmy days, that the British found extant in the Punjab in 1846. Rather, what we find are the relics of ancient systems or institutions that had survived the stress of disruption, anarchy, internecine feuds, and foreign invasions. The Sikh education—Vernacular Education in Gurmukhi,—may be said to have been in its infancy, but Gurmukhi yet needed development and elevation to the level of a standard language as a vehicle for the expression of ideas—its laurels were, if ever at all, yet to be won.

However poorly the actual might correspond to the ideal, it is worthy of note that, both among Hindus and Muhammadans, many teachers "instructed for their own pleasure, or what is more likely, under the idea that they were engaged in a meritorious and laudable task."[1] Similarly, for educational purposes, a combination was visible among the residents of the village, and "the general acknowledgment of the moral obligation of education."[1]

Mass Education.—The indigenous system of education in vogue in the Punjab in 1846 may now be briefly described. As regards mass education, the school was an institution which a village community was expected to maintain as a matter of course. The State, by encouraging and patronising men of light and learning, supplied the initiative, and it rendered material help to the village schools in the form of freehold grants. It is our personal opinion that the Hindu ideal did not look upon secular education as something apart from, and quite independent of, religion or religious education. For them, the latter formed the natural complement to the former which, in its turn, was a preliminary acquisition essential for a sound religious education. According to the Vedas from

[1]Punjab Records, 25th February, 1854.

which the earliest Aryan educational system drew its inspiration, science did not militate against religion: in India the parallel to the persecutions of Roger Bacon or Gallileo does not exist. The various advanced arts and sciences, *e.g.*, the Science of War, of Music, of Medicine, and of Mechanics or Engineering, were not treated as things apart from religion but as mere parts of the religious system: they were the *Up-Vedas*, the class of writings subordinate to the Vedas, known respectively as the Dhanur-Veda, Gandharve-Veda, Ayur-Veda and Sthapatya-Veda, emanating, in order, from the Yajur, Sama, Rig and Athervana Vedas. The Mohammadan whose ideal of life and polity was pre-dominently theocratic laid stress chiefly upon the study of the Koran and the Hadis—the sayings and teachings of the Prophet. To a Sikh, as a member of the ruling class, education in addition to what the Hindu schools might give him access to meant the study of the Granth as well as "learning to ride and being a warrior," although, it may be remarked in passing, that the ordinary Sikh child was averse to learning the multiplication table—an illustration of the low regard in which commercial classes and commercial education were held by the rulling class.

The various institutions answered to the aims briefly sketched above. Pathshalas, Koran schools, and Gurmukhi schools were respectively Hindu, Muslim, and Sikh institutions chiefly or entirely devoted to the propagation of religious teaching. Elementary knowledge of Shastras was imparted or Mantras learnt; the Koran was repeated and learnt, chiefly by rote, and Saadis' Pand-Nama recited; Gurmukhi character was taught and practice in the study of the Granth or portions thereof acquired.

The Chatsalas, *i.e.,* Mahajani and Lande schools ministered to the wants of the trading community. In these schools, the Padha (if a Hindu) or the Mian (if a Muslim) taught his young pupils mental arithmetic, learning to count mentally and how to keep business-correspondence and Behi-khata. This skill at accounts while not much mental discipline can be claimed for it, was a few years afterwards the object of much praise on the part of British authorities who came in contact with the village accountant.[1]

Persian was the official language in both Muhammadan and Sikh times. It was indeed the language of the literate—the lingua franca of the official class. The necessary instruction was provided by maktabs, Persian-Koran schools, and Persian schools. The teachers were almost invariably Muhammadans, but as these schools were primarily meant for the intelligensia and inasmuch as Persian had a definite value in terms of livelihood and Government employment, Hindus attended them as freely as Muhammadans. Writing was taught, and standard Persian works, especially Saadis' Gulistan and Bostan which formed the subjects of study were much enjoyed. It may be mentioned that Persian schools were considered by the British authorities a few years later, to be "the most genuinely educational institutions in the country."[2]

School were generally attached to mosques, temples, or dharamsalas, and the same contribution of land or money often supported both the institutions. They were also held in huts of faqirs or at the houses of liberal persons. Occasionally, the accountant engaged by a wealthy Zamindar in a village in

---

[1]Punjab Records, April, 1855.

[2]Punjab Education Report 1856-57, paragraph 16.

order to teach his sons taught also other boys of the village.

The state, as already remarked, helped schools by allotment. In some cases, the teacher was remunerated for his services with the annual grant of 50 maunds of gain, or by a funod derived from the cess of a certain amount of grain five seers on every plough. The system of regular fees was not in favour, but weekly gifts were made to the teacher who also received donations from parents, on festivals, marriages, and other auspicious occasions in the pupil's family. Thy average income of a teacher has been variously estimated. According to a statement made by Mr. Montgomery, Commissioner, Lahore Division, in 1850, the average salaries of masters ran from Re. 1-2-0 to Rs. 8-8-0 per mensem, while Dr. Leitner puts the monthly income of Padhas at Rs.50 on an average, sometimes at even Rs. 100 per mensem. The right amount may be fixed somewhere between these extermes, but it may be quite safely asserted that, because the teacher was also generally the priest or Mullah his status, the respect he might command and indirectly his remuneration were all determined by the reputation he enjoyed for his learning, character, and his interest as a priest in the well-being of his flock. In a word, public opinion, not an appointment order issued by the State or the village council, determined his deserts and his living wage. Consequently, side by side with teachers who barely eked out a precarious living, there were to be found others (fewer of course) of the same profession who enjoyed a degree of affluence which enabled them even to provide food and residence for some of there poorer pupils.

Such were the arrangements for elementary education taht existed in the Punjab at this period. As stated before, the moral obligation of education was generally recognised and parents were expected to send their children to one institution or another. Unlike other parts of Hindustan, in most districts of the Punjab, it was discovered "that all classes, agricultural and non-agricultural, manifested a desire for education."[1]

Higher Education.—As regards education of an advanced character, there is not much to relate. The atmosphere of chaos and insecurity that had generally been the order of the day was not conducive to the progress of learning, let alone higher learnlng: in fact, the education to be found in the Punjab—apart from religious instruction—was strictly of a practical or or utilitarian character. However, the inspiring influence of traditional reverence for learning was still there and the aim of education as the means of culture was not entirely lost sight of. Those, selected few of course, aspiring to knowledge for its own sake could still find teachers and institutions to help them. Philosophy, astronomy, astrology, even medicine was taught in Hindu secular schools of various kinds. The Muhammadan Madrassas—religions and secular –taught Theology, Fiqah, astronomy, and the *Yunani* system of medicine. The Sikh seats of learning—*e.g.*, Amritsar Akalbunga, Damdma Dharmsala in Raipur – testified to the ardour for *Jhana* (divine knowledge) evinced by their pupils. The teachers were generally men of eminence ; they not only imparted free education, but provided their disciples with shelter, food, and clothing. While unber instruction, the pupils were not as a rule expected to make any presents to their teacher, though personal service on their part was here, as in the case of scholars of junior

---

[1]Punjab Administration Report, 1848-50.

grades, considered to be a mark of grace and was freely given and accepted.

Female Education.—The education imparted to females was almost entirely of a religious or semi-religious character. The Punjabi was not opposed to female education but, considering the home to be the only proper sphere for woman, he was content of she could recite the Koran, read the Granth or Janam Sakhi, or study the Ramayana or Bhagwad-Gita at home. Muhammadan girls generally read the Koran at the mosque school along with the young boys there; Sikh girls attended Dharamsalas; while Hindu girls mostly received their education at home. The teacher was generally the Mullah, the bhai, or the family priest, though female teachers—Hindu, Muslim and Sikh—were also to be found.

Summary: General Features.—So much about the native system of education in its outline. Coming to the number of schools, of pupils under instruction, and the percentage of scholars to population or childern of school-going age, it is not possible to speak with completeness or certainty. There is a great paucity of records of all kinds and those available are either incomplete or conflicting. Mr. Arnold in his Educational Report for 1856-57 estimates the number of boys attending indigenous schools, deducting those attending Koran and Lande schools at 24,968; the Education Report for 1878-79 at 53,207; according to the census 1881-82, the lowest number of scholars attending Indigenous schools was 60,168, "but," says Dr. Leitner in his "Indigenous Education in the Punjab." "in reality it could not have been less than 96,585. In 1882-83 when full information was obtained, by the desire of His Honour the Lieutenant Governor, as to the number of indigenous schools, there were **13,109** schools of all kinds with **133,588** scholars. It need not be pointed out that ever since **1856**, when the departmental system was established, the number of indigenous schools, for reasons to be noted at another place, had been steadly going down. According to the investigations made by Sir John Lawrence in **1849-50**, "the numbers were found to vary from one school to every **1,783** inhabitants to one school to every **1441**—according to Munro's rough calculation (*i.e.*, taking boys of school-going age to be 6 per cent of population), this will give, for the Punjab—reckoning ten booys to each school—one boy attending school to every nine of the proper age, for the North-West Provinces, now known as tbe United Provinces of Agra and Oudh, one boy in every eighteen. If we add the number of female childern under tuition, it will not appreciably affect this estimate."[1] This last estimate, the result of the earliest authentic enquiry, may be safely accepted, for it errs, if at all, on the side of incomepleteness, as figures for the Leiah and Peshawar Divisions are not included in and because it is not likely that, during the three years which elapsed between 1846-49—the period of the Sikh Wars—any appreciable number of new schools sprung into existence.

Before taking leave of this part of our subject, it seems necessary to review briefly the merits and drawbacks of the system of education outlined above. An historian is not expected to be also a philosopher, but he has to trace the development of events or movements and a review of the essential features likely to help or retard progress cannot be entirely beyond his sphere.

---

[1]F. W. Thomas : The History and Prospects of British Education in India, page 13.

Most of the useful features of the indigenous system of education have already been alluded to in the foregoing narrative. For instance, reference has been made to the influence of public opinion upon the status of and regard enjoyed by the village teacher. A direct corollary of this was the co-operation between the teacher and the parent. There were no fines for absence or neglect and no home-task as distinguished from voluntary study at home According to a high authority, "Education to be morally effective must rest on a religous foundation,"[1] and under this old system education and religion were not incompatibles ; a teacher in the discharge of his duties was practising dharma or fuifilling a religious obligation. There was thus a personal bond between the teacher and his pupil and its effect upon the latter's character may be easily eastimated

We may now look at the matter from the other side. This side is indeed more important for a student of history. Education as the British found it in the Punjab was their raw material for work ; and before any measures could be devised to continue, develop, or improve it, a thorough knowledge of the direction in which it needed, or was capable of, improvement was essential. In judging indigenous education from this standpoint, we must not be understood to be a pplying a standard of another age or one much in advance of the times. What was being actually done by the British in Bengal or North-Western Provinces—formerly parts, like the Punjab, of the Sultanate of Delhi—ought to have been possible of attainment and generally achieved here in the Punjab by any enlightened government.

To note the chief shortcoming succinctly. Indigenous Educa-

---

[1]**The Education of India—Mayhew, page 210.**

tion was cheap and within easy reach, but the quality of instruction imported was generally far from satisfactory. While religious education was rightly considered to constitute an important factor in human life secular education was denied the importance it deserved. Learning was held in great respect, but learning often implied religious learning, a knowledge of philosophy, metaphysics, cultivation of a spirit of religious enquiry, and, it may be, of appreciation of poetry. But history, geography, physical science, and mechanics had no place in that system. It was very rarely that a Panjabi scholar of learning interested himself in the study of Politics or Political Economy. Mass education imparted, as as already noted, is the form of arithmetical tables, system of accounts writing practised by some classes even to the extent of an art, and recitation of verses from the Kamla, of course meant useful, practical knowledge, but there was no attempt at training every boy's faculties, or developing in him a sense of the beautiful by teaching, him drawing, etc., and a mention of gardening, manual training, or elementary hygiene or agriculture would have simply astounded the parent and the teacher alike. Under these circmstances, it is not a harsh verdict to pass that the mental outlook of an average Punjabi was painfully narrow and circumscribed.

A glance at the methods of work does not materially affect the observations made above. Teaching was considered as a meritorious work and as such, every one was good enough to teach boys and no apprenticeship or training was required for it. Hence the art of economy of time or effort was not much regarded. All though small knots of boys received their lessons together in some of the books, yet there was no system of classes, nor teaching boys in divisions according to their different attainments. It cannot be stated in reply that teaching was indvidualistic, because the teacher could hardly attend to a boy for more than a few minutes during the day the greater part of which the latter naturally spent in "going over his lessons," when he might be occasionally helped by another older but equally raw boy. There was, moreover, no system or practice of checking the teacher's work either by the State authorities or the Village or Town Panchayat; no standard of educational efficiency was therefore set, and it is not strange that the avertage village teacher was a dull unprogressive plodder who depended more upon the use of his rod than his brains to mak his pupils learn.

Having taken stock of our educational assets, it now remains for us to see what use the British Government made of the situation. Its methods and achievements it is the object of the following chapters to relate.

3

Education in the early yeras of British Rule.

As remarked in a previous chapter, Government was during this period busy setting up the machinery of its administration, and the defence of the country and pacification of the people occupied most of its attention. This need not be taken to mean that, as in the later Moghul or the Sikh periods, the subject of education was thrown in to the background to be taken up when Government had nothing else to occupy it. It simply implies that, pending the information about the educational state of the people, no comprehensive scheme was taken in hand and no lump sum provided for educational purposes from the imperial revenues. The District Officers—the Indian Civil Service—were expected to be aware of their traditions and to devise means for the education and up-lift of the people under their charge. Not that the later developments have relieved the district authorities of their responsibility in this direction. But the Civil Officers of the period under consideration had no definite policy, promulgated either by the Imperial or the provincial Government, to direct their measures, and as such much more depended upon the interest taken in educational matters by them in their individual capacity than it does to-day.

Before taking up the details of progress during this period, it may be noted that of the various Indian provinces the Punjab was one of the last to be annexed by the British Government. The effect upon education of this rather very late annexation was very peculiar. The principal educational aims and the fundamental principles of the educational policy of the government had already been formulated and decided upon in relation to its work in other provinces previous to the annexation of the Punjab. To illustrate ; in 1829, in a Government letter, Lord William Bentinck stated the settled policy of the Government in the following words :—

"It was the wish and admitted policy of the British Government to rend its own language gradually and eventually the language of public business throughout the country."[1] His famous proclamation of March 1835, which promulgated that the chief aim of the educational policy should be to promote a knowledge of European literature and science and that all funds appropriated for the purpose of education would henceforth be employed in imparting the native population a knowledge of English literature and science through the medium of English language, was a measure the importance of which can hardly be over-rated and the far-reaching consequences whereof it is not possible to gauge in their entirety. Time whose comment will always be the truest soon exposed the "utter impracticability of the view of those who thought that the English language should be

[1]Education and Statemanship in India—by James, Chapter 2.

almost entirely maintained by the Christian Missionaries. Besides these, there were, in addition to the Kot Garh school mentioned already, three elementary schools at Ambala Cantonment, at Kangra and at Jandiala in the Amritsar District. In the field of female education missionary societies were much ahead of the Government, because, while female education formed no part of the official programme during this period, the American Presbyterian Mission, Ludhiana, set up its first elementary school for females, as early as 1836[1] and the Church Missionary Orphanage was opened at Amritsar in 1853.

As mentioned already, all these institutions were maintained by the various missionary societies and no financial aid was rendered to them by Government. This should not be taken to mean that Government did not appreciate the educational value and importance of these schools. On the other hand, in 1852, Government, with the full concurrence of Captain Brown, Depty Commissioner, Ambala, made over to the American Presbyterian Mission the indigenous school at Ambala City, because, "the Board was of opinion that the missionaries would do more justice to the institution than would be possible, were it managed by the Civil Officers of the Government."[2] The land for school houses was also made over in free gift and interest on the money in deposit was to paid to them. The reason why Government did not render such schools regular financial help was because till 1854 the orders of the Court of Directors forbade "grants of

[1] Cis-Sutlej Territory under British protection and influence by the Treaty of Amritsar, 1809.

[2] Punjab Records, May 1852.

money in aid of secular education carried on in schools established and conducted by Christian Missonaries."[1]

To resume the narrative of education under the Government. The first educational question of importance, which was at the same time an administrative question, was about the official language and the language or languages to be taught in schools. It was of course necessary to decide in which language the government work—revenue, judicial, etc.,—was to be carried on. Similarly the vernacular language or language to be studied in schools were to be determined, so that European knowledge and science—the aim of education as set forth in 1835 and subsequently pertially modified in 1840—might be taught through the medium of the vernacular. Too many vernaculars would evidently mean waste of effort and the perpetuation of petty divisions among the people. Decision on both these points was soon arrived at. After the linguistic condition of the province had been duly considered it was decided that Urdu was to replace Persian as the court language for the transaction of public business though the change was to be brought about gradually so as prevent any hardship to the people. Correspondence between high officers of State was of course to be carried on in English. Urdu was declared to be the official language in the Multan Division in 1851, in Hazara in 1853, and in the Leiah and Peshawar divisions in 1854. In some cases, the use of Persian side by side with Urdu was allowed for a year more from the date of orders. The transition was complete througout the province by the end of 1855.

---

[1] Minute by Lord Dalhousie, 1854, Thirteenth Section.

As regards the language or languages to be taught in schools, it was felt that Punjabi, "though of sacred origin, and in the days of Sikh supremacy both a courtly and a priestly tongue, was now rapidly falling into desuetude"[1] and was "degenerating into a mere provincial or rude dialect; whereas Urdu or Hindustani—was becoming familiar to the upper and middle classes and the ruder population understood it nearly as well as their fellow-subjects in Hindustan."[1] The Persian and Urdu languages were to be taught in schools under the patronage of Government, though the chief language to be used was Urdu with the Persian character, because this language was "becoming more than a lingua franca."[2] The Court of Directors also, in their Despatch No. 43 of 1855, endorsed the suggestion of Mr. Mcleod, Judicial Commissioner, Punjab, that "Urdu... be made familiar, in the first instance, to the educated classes, and through them, as would certainly follow, to the entire body of the people, to the eventual supersession of inferior local dialects." Urdu was therefore to be the medium of instruction in schools under government control or patronage.

Coming to the educational institutions established by the Government during this period, it may be pointed out that schools were not graded, like present day schools, as High Schools, Middle Schools, or Primary Schools. There was at this time no Government or private University in India and no Entrance or Matriculation Examination. Nor was there any accepted classification of schools, marking off the various kinds of schools distinctly from one another. The broad divisions may, however, be noted, *viz.*, Zillah Schools located

1 Punjab Administration Report, 1851-52, 1852-53, page 184.
2 *Ibid* 1854-56, pages 45.

at the head quarters of the various districts, where English was a subject of instruction and an education of a higher class was generally provided ; and schools situated at Tahsil towns or in the interior of districts where the education imparted was strictly of an elementary character, though provision for the study of English existed in some places.

The first Government school in the Punjab territory was that opened at Simla on 1st March, 1848, by Mr. Edwardes, Superintendent, Hill States. Another school at Hoshiarpur was opened the same year by Colonel Abbott. The former was maintained from Imperial revenues, and the latter from contributions made by zamindars in the form of a certain percentage on their revenue for the support of schools. Mr. Edwardes also opened in the same year thirteen District Schools with 213 scholars on the rolls. This was before 1849, when the annexation of the Punjab took place.

In 1849, the Deputy Commissioner, Amritsar, proposed the establishment of a Government school at Amritsar, Rs. 5,000 per annum were sanctioned from Imperial revenues and the school was opened in May, 1851. Other Zillah schools were established at Rawalpindi, Gujrat, Shahpur, Multan, Jheleum and Jullundur, so that towards the close of 1854 there were eight schools undor thc Government in which education of a higher standard than an elementary education was imparted. The Amritsar school was the best of these schools.[1] The subjects of study in these schools included English, Geometry and Geography.

Besides these schools situated at the head quarters or central stations of various districts, there were eleven schools

[1] This school was, however, soon after entrusted to the American Mission.

at Tahsil towns or in the interior of the district in Hoshiarpur district, three schools at Tahsil towns in Shahpur district; four schools in Gujrat district established by Mr. Temple ; two schools in the Jhelum district ; two schools in the Multan district besides a school at Gugera[1] established by Captain Reid ; and a school at Fatehjang in the Rawalpindi district or twenty-four schools in all[2]. All these schools were established by the District Officers between 1851 and 1854. We may call these institutions by the name of elementary schools where the three R's. were taught, though provision for the study of English was also often made and Persian which was popular with the people was also taught in most schools.

During this period, Delhi territory formed a Part of the North-Western Provinces now known as the United Provinces. It was transferred to the Punjab Administration after the Mutiny in February, 1858. The review made above does not consequently take into account the state of education there.

As noticed above incidentally, various institutions established by the District officers were under the control of the Government, but were not generally maintained from imperial revenues. In fact, the Government schools at Amritsar and Simla were the only schools in the Punjab supported by government out of the general revenues[3]. Other schools were maintained out of local funds. For instance, the school at Rawalpindy was maintained by a grant-in-aid from the surplus of town duty proceeds. An Educational cess, with the consent

---

[1] See Mr. Arnold's report for 1856-57, paragraphs 5, 6. Schools at Ferozepore and Sialkot were established in 1856 and are included in the above narrative.

[2] See Mr. Arnold's Report, 1856-57, para. 6.

[3] Now Montgomery.

of the people, was levied in most distrcts, *e.g*, in Hoshiarpur, Gujrat and Sialkot districts. In other districts, *e..g*, Jullundur, schools were maintained out of Nazul funds and the Nazrana fund was made use of in other places.

The number of scholars on the rolls or of daily attendance at these schoools are unfortunately not available. It my be assumed however, that most of these schools were popular and well-attended, seeing that they were founded only in districts and at places where the District authorities felt a real interest in education and who, therefore, might be expected to see that these schools were kept in a flourishing condition. The general educational condition of the province is thus summarised in the Administration Report, 1854-55, 1855-56. "It would probably be permature to direct any very strenuous efforts at present upon English Education. The trials that have heretofore been made in the Punjab have not been very successful. It may be better to rest a while until a class of youths shall have risen fit to receive the higher European learning by means of the English language. The great and immediate object for attainment it the imparting of sound elementary knowledge in the verancular form."

As regards indigenous schools, it may be generally stated that they continued to work as usual during this period. According to the Administration Report, 1854-55, 1855-56, there were in the Punjab 3,372 indigenous schools, with 31,592 scholars. A note is also made of the useful purpose served by these institutions in the following words occurring in the same report. "The style of education is of course most primitive........But the majority of people, though ignorant, are yet not insensible to the blessings of knowledge of their children."

It was stated in the introduction to this work that although during this period no education scheme on a comprehensive basis was taken in hand, yet the educational possibilities of the province were explored and a programme of operations for the future was prepared. Here too, as explained at some length in the opening paragraphs of this chapter, the experience acquired in the field of education in the contiguous North-Western Provinces—was avilable for use in the Punjab. Mr. Thomason, the Lieutenant-Governor of the North-Western Provinces from 1843—1853, was deeply interested in the education of the people under his charge; a scheme of elementary education drawn up by him was finally approved by the Supreme Government and the Court of Directors, and had been in operation, since 1850, in the eight districts of the North-Western Provinces as an experimental measure. While the Government was to encourage the existing indigenous schools to improve themselves, schools under direct state control and management were to be opened on what came commonly to be known as the *Halqa Bandi* system. The plan was this "A pargannah being chosen, it was ascertained how many children of a school-going-age it numbered, what revenue it paid, and what expense it could therefore bear. A cluster of villages, some four or five, was then marked out and the most central of the villages fixed upon as the site of the school." These schools were to be maintained by means of an educational cess levied upon the zamindars equal to one per cent. of the revenue payable by them. The course of studies included reading and writing the vernacular languages, bothe Urdu and Hindi, accounts and the mensuration of land according to the indigenous system. Instruction in Geography, Geometry, or other general subjects, conveyed through the medium of the vernacular languages, was to be arranged for if the people desired it. There was, in addition, a Government village school at the head quarters of every Tahsildar. Visitors were appointed to inspect and report on these schools, the highest eductional officer being designated as the Visitor-general.

We have described the scheme of this experiment in some detail, because three years later, when in 1853 the experiment was pronounced to be a success and the Government of the North-Western Provinces submitted a proposal for the extension of the scheme of village schools to the remaining districts of the province, the Supreme Government recommended that the "Punjab Government should consider whether the system of Vernacular education in the North-Western Provinces might not be beneficially introduced lnto the Punjab."[1] The subject of education occupied therefore the earnest attention of the Government. It was ascertained that there was "less prejudice and fewer elements of passive hindrance or active opposition here than elsewhere. The upper classes displayed a candid intelligence and inquisitiveness in respect of Asiatic learning and European science"[1] and the agricultural classes, too, were not hopelessly apathetic. The Punjab, it was considered, was ripe for the introduction of an educational scheme.

It was further resolved that the North-Western System of uernacular education, outlined above, was well adapted for

[1] Punjab Administration Report, 1851-52, 1852-53, page 183.

the Punjab. A scheme, embodying the following main proposals was consequently prepared and submitted for sanction in May, 1854 :—

(1) The establishment of fifty schools at Tahsil Towns and Normal Schools for training teachers for the same.

(2) The appointment of a Visitor-general and twelve zillah and fifty Purganah visitors.

(3) The establishment of a Central College at Lahore.

The scheme thus contemplated, as in the case of the North-Western Provinces scheme outlined in a letter (of that Government), dated the 19th April, 1843, the establishment of one Government School, as a model, at each Tahsil town and providing an agency for visting all the native schools which might consent to Government inspection, and for furnishing the people and the teachers with advice, assistance and encouragement.

The Supreme Government sanctioned this scheme with certain modifications and Lord Dalhousie in his minute, dated the 6th June 1854 solicited "the sanction of the Hon' ble Court to the introduction of the proposed system of vernacular edacation into the Punjab including prospectively the foundation of a College at Lahore." The annual expenditure to be incurred by the State was not to exceed one lakh of rupees. The approval of the Court of Directors was also obtained in due course.[1]

The scheme, though a modest measure, was yet a distinct advance upon the existing conditions, but it was not destined

---

[1] Punjba Admainstration Report, 1854-55, page 70.

to reach the final stage of being put into practice. What circumstances prevented its consummation will form the subject of the narrative in the next chapter.

4

Second period : —1854—1884—I.

Despatches of 1854 and 1859.

In 1852-53, when the question of the renewal of the charter of the East India Company came before the British Parliament, a parliamentry enquiry into the Indian affairs was ordered to be held, as had been the custom. For reasons on which it is not necessary to dwell here, the question of education was one of the most important question discussed before the Lords, Committee in 1852-53. Many petitions were presented to Parliament and eminent witnesses-statesmen, missionaries and educationists gave their views on the various problems and aspects of education, *viz.* High Schools, Universities, Religious Instruction, and Elementary Education.

The outcome of the keen interest envinced in education was the issue by the Court of Directors, soon after the control of Indian affairs was again vested in them, of the educational despatch of 1854, which has since been described as "the Magna Charta of English Education in India." The quote from the minute of Lord Dalhousie on the despatch, "It contained a scheme of education for all India, far wider and more comprehensive than the Local or the Supreme Gorvenment could ever have ventured to suggest."[1] "The educational system elaborated in the despatch was indeed, both in its character and scope, far in advance of anything existing at the time, of its inception. It furnished, in fact, a masterly and comprehensive outlined, the filling up of which was necessarily to be the work of many years."[2]

An abstract of the despatch many now be given. The Despatch of 1854 invited the special attention of the Government of India to the improvement and far wider exetnsion of education, both English and Vernacular. The means prescribed for the attainment of these objects were:—(1) the constiution of a separate department of the administration for education, (2) the institution of Universities at the presidency tswns; (3) the establishment of institutions of training teachers of all classes of schools. The existing Gorvernment Colleges and High Shools were to be maintained, and new ones opened where necessary. New middle schools were to be established and more attention was to be given to vernacular schools indigenous or otherwise, for elementary education. Lastly, a system of grants-in-aid was to be introduced to encourage and aid private enterprise in the cause of education.

A few concluding remarks are necessary in this connection. The aim of education remained the same as heretofore, *i.e.*, "the diffusion of the improved arts, scince, philosophy, and literature of Europe; in short of European knowledge."[3]

---

[1] Selctions from Educational Records 1840-59, page 364.
[2] Resolution of the Government of India, appointing the Indian Education Commission quoted by Sayyad Mahmood in his English Education in India, page 85.
[3] The Despatch of 1854, para. 7.

The medium of instruction, however, was to be for the masses the vernacular, though the use of English was to continue as the most perfect medium for the eduation of the persons who had acquired a sufficient knowledge of it to receive general instuction through it. The change in the medim of instruction was, it may be noted, thus definitely recognisd and authoritativevely pronounced by the Government. Before 1854, the subject of vernacular education had not received the full amount of attention which it deserved. The broad line of separation which then existed between schools in which the medoia for imparting instruction differed was to be done away with and the aglnovernacular and vernacular middle schools were to be included in the same class. A system of scholarship tenable in colleges, high schools and lower schools was to be insttiuted to encourage and reward the promising student of high schools, middle schools, and village or primary schools respectively and to connect lower schools with higher schools and higher schools with colleges. Female education was henceforth to be cordially supported by Government. Lastly, the principle of religious neutrality was again affirmed, though the Bible, as before, was to be placed in the libraries of the colleges and schools and the pupils were allowed to discuss it freely.

In the light of the above, the educational scheme under consideration in the Punjab was of course looked upon as limited and inadequate, and fresh measures were therefore proposed to carry out the intentions of the desaptch. The annual cost to be borne by Government was not to exceed three lakhs.

Before taking up the story of these measures, we may refer to the Secretary of State's Despatch of 1859 which constitutes the second important document on which India Education is based. It was received soon after the control of Indian Administration had been taken over by the Crown as a result of the Mutiny of 1857. It reviewed "the progress made under the earlier despatch, which it re-iterated and confirmed with a single exception, as to the course to be adopted for promoting elementary edcation."[1] The grant-in-aid system—to be discussed later on—had not proved successful in its application to schools of the lower class, although it had been freely availed of by those of higher class. It was therefore suggested in the Despatch that "the means of elementary education should be provided by the direct instrumentality of the officers of Government."[2] In the Punjab as we shall see later on, the intentions of the despatch in this respect had already been anticipated.

Of the subesquent despatches of 1864 and 1866 by Sir Charles Wood and Lord De Grey and Ripon respectively it is not necessary to speak here ; they supported and amplified the two great despatches detailed above.

The period under consideration was, as already stated, one of great activity and development in the field of education, with which we shall deal in the present and the succeeding chapters under the following heads: Administrative Machinery, Financial Arrangements, Grants-in-aid, Primary Education, Secondary Education, Colleges and the Punjab University, Female Education, Training of Teachers, Special Education and Accessory Measures and External Agencies

[1] Indain Education Commission on the Despatch of 1859, quoted by F. Thomas in his Hist. and Prospects of Br. Ed. in India, page 62.
[2] Despatch of 1859 paragraph 50.

due to and for the extension of education. The work of the Indian Education Commission and the effect of its recommendations upon the Punjab will be considered in a separate chapter.

(*1*) *Administrative Machinery.*—The Punjab Education Department was instituted in January, 1856. The appointment of a Director-General on Rs. 1,200 per mensem was sanctioned, and an inspection staff consisting of two inspectors on Rs.600 of each, ten Deputy Inspectors each receiving a salary between Rs. 80 and Rs. 150 per mensem, and seventeen Sub-Deputy Inspectors on salaries of Rs. 20 to Rs. 60 was also to be appointed. The designations, Deputy Inspector and Sub-Deputy Inspector, were to be used instead of *Zillah* and Pargunnah Visitors, as the officers appointed in the Punjab held each the educational charge of two or there districts and purgannahs respectively.

In the despatch of 1854, it was recommended by the Court of Directors that "the first heads of the Educational Department, as well as some of the inspectors, should be members of our Civil Service, as such appointments—would tend to raise the estimation in which these officers would be held, and to show the importance we attached to the subject of education." In pursuance of the above, Mr. Arnold who was an Assistant Commissioner in the Punjab was appointed Director of Public Instruction in January, 1856. The two European Inspectors were in charge of the Eastern and Western Circles into which the Province was divided for the purposes of education. As regards the appointment of eleven Deputy Inspectors (for the hill district of Kangra was soon given a separate Deputy Inspector) and seventeen Sub-Deputy Inspectors, a sufficient number of Punjabis competent to discharge these duties was not available and foreigners from Hindustan had to be taken. The Department continued to be under the control of the Financial Commissioner.

Before the organisation of the Department, the various schools maintained out of the Imperial revenues or local cesses had been under the control of the Civil Officers. A uniform local cess of one per cent[1] for educational purposes had also been introduced throughout the province in the beginning of 1855. The control of all Government institutions was now as a matter of course transferred to the Education Department under the Director, though some District Officers who wished to keep in their own hands the expenditure of the school cess and the organisation of village schools were reluctant to hand over the schools to the Department.

The evils resulting from this dissociation of the educational department from the civil authorities soon became manifest. In 1858, the Chief Commissioner remarked that in many places a want of vitality and of quickening power in the system was perceptible. In the districts of Sialkot, Amritsar

---

[1] The payment of the cess was, in most cases, entered as one of sums payable by the village community in the Settlement papers, but in some districts where the settlements had been concluded, it was introduced afterwards.

Where the cess was introduced after the settlement had been completed, it was optional with the zamindars to consent to, or to decline its payment. But not so, when the revision of settlement took place.

The cess was clearly a local fund and the amount collected in a district was expended in the same district. By the measures of 1873-74 (See Page 33) the cess was amalgamated into the District Fund.

and Gujranwala, for instance, the principal schools were numerically less attended than before. And thus by permiting the District Officers to be unconcerned in schools, the Government lost much of that *moral influence* which it might ligitimately exert in favour of education."[1]

The drawbacks too arising from the appointment of foreign Deputy and Sub-Deputy Inspectors were not late to appear. The majority of them were not very capable officers as "only third-rate men found it worth their while to take service far from their homes," and they had very little influence with the people. So, although the inspection staff had been strengthened by the appointment of a third European inspector for the Delhi territory which was transferred to the Punjab administration in February, 1858, yet the supervision of schools committed to the charge of Indian assistants was found to be very inefficient.

The despatch of 1859 had also drawn attention to the excessive cost of the administration of educational departments as compared with the expenditure on the direct work of instruction and desired the provincial Governments to review the existing establishments.[2]

A radical reform was therefore carried out towards the close of 1859-60. The Indian supervising agency was abolished and the executive management of Vernacular schools was placed in the hands of District Officers. Several capable Deputy and Sub-Deputy Inspectors were, however, retained on reduced salaries under the District Officers ; they were to

[1] Punjab Records, December 1858,—letter No. 2654, dated 15th December 1858, from the Chief Commissioner, Punjab, to the Financial Commisioner.
[2] Despatch of 1859, paragraph 40.

do, under the new name of District Moharrirs, the office work connected with charge of the schools. Next year, because it had been found that many of the Tahsildars were not competent to conduct a proper examination even of elementary schools, a qualified official was appointed under each district officer for supervising the educational needs of these schools. The Moharrirs were to be paid out of the district educational cess fund. Finally the Director of Public Instruction was placed in direct communication with the Government.

The new measures answered their purpose and endured to the close of our period; and the later developments consequent on the extension of education and on the increase in the number of educational institutions may now be briefly summarised. A fourth Inspector of Schools was appointed for the Frontier Circle in 1863-64 and a redistribution of the districts was consequently made among the four Inspectors who in 1884 held the charge of Ambala, Lahore, Rawalpindi, and Frontier (know also as Multan) Circles. These arrangements were slightly modified in 1883-84, when in accordance with the recommendation of the Bengal Committee that the inspection of all European Schools should be entrusted to a single officer in order to ensure uniformity of treatment, the inspection of all such schools in the Punjab was made over to the Inspector of the Lahore Circle and the necessary redistribution of Circles among the Inspectors effected. An Indian Deputy Inspector for each Circle had also been appointed in 1863-64.

Besides the abov-mentioned higher officers, an Indian Inspecting officer, called Chief Schools Moharrir, was kept in each district that could afford it. His salary which was to be paid out of the local education cess varied from Rs. 30 to Rs. 70 per mensem in various districts. These Chief Schools Moharrirs were highly useful public servants, but they were inferior both in attainments and in social position to the standard it was desirable that men discharging so important duties should maintain. Consequently, from 1870-71 onward, they were gradually replaced by District Inspecors on higher salaries, *i.e.*, Rs. 100 per mensem or upwards. The cost of subordinate inspection was transferred to Provincial Services in 1873-74. Up to 1876-77, there were fourteen District Inspectors, one District Inspectress, and sixteen Chief School Moharrirs. The new scheme sanctioned the same year provided for twenty District Inspectors, one District Inspectress (appointed in 1868-69), ten Chief Moharrirs, and the salaries and propspects of the whole staff were improved.

To enlist popular support for the work and progress of elementary schools, local Committees of Public Instruction began to be formed in various districts from 1864-65 ; and village Committees were also organized at different localities. However, with a few exceptions, where some activity was visible on account of the solicitude of the Civil authorities, these non-official committees did not yet display much interest in the cause of education commended to their care.

(2) *Financial Arrangements.*—The sources of revenue from which all educational charges were met fall under two heads : Provincial or Imperial Revenues and Local sources, the most important of which till 1871 was the one per cent education cess levied on zamindars equal to one per cent of the land-

revenue due from them. The income fees, subscriptions, and endowments may also be included in the second class.

As narrated in the foregoing section, Provincial revenues and Local cesses (or cesses from 1871) were administered respectively by the Director of Public Instruction and the District Officers and we have now to indicate broadly the manner in which these were expended.

Up to 1859-60 inclusive Village schools situated in the interior of district were maintained out of the Educational Cess. "But the Village Schools did not absorb the entire yield of this cess and fixed quotas were paid for Office Establishments, maintenance of Normal Schools, salaries of Extra Sub-Deputy Inspectors of supervision of Villages Schools, and also towards defraying the cost of publishing the Sarkari Akhbar."[1] All other charges—Direction, Inspection, Zillah Schools, Tahsils Schools, Grants-in-aid were provided from Imperial revenues.

After the reform measures carried out the same year, the cost of the maintenance of the subordinate inspection staff, if any, and of Tahsils Schools was also transferred to the Educational Cess, so that more money might be found from Imperial Revenues for the opening of High and Middle Schools. In other words Government was to provide chiefly for Higher School or Middle School education while the people themselves were to find money for elementary education. In adherence to this principle, superior Tahsil Schools—known as Town Schools from 1862-63—were to be supported by Government

[1] Punjab Records, September 1859. The cost of the Sarkari Akhbar was however defrayed from Imperial Revenues from April 1864.

from Imperial revenues from the next year.

These arrangements continued till the close of 1871-72, except that the Municipal Committees instituted in 1866-67 were authorised to expend a part of their funds on education. The contribution made by the Educational Cess to the popular education bears a satisfactory comparison with the expenditure from Imperial revenues—amounting to about one-third or one-half of the latter as would be clear from the following figures :—

Year.	Expenditure from Imperial Revenues.	Expenditure from cess Fund.	REMARKS
	Rs.	Rs.	
1856-57	1,05,392	23,472	Savings of Rs. 1,14,572 in deposit.
1860-61	1,45,912	2,15,510	Savings of Rs. 13,691 in deposit.
1864-65	4,14,759	2,75,512	
1868-69	5,96,807	2,23,512	
1871-72	6,16,354	2,11,459	Savings of Rs. 4,863 in deposit.

The decentralisation of finances was carried out by the Supreme Government in 1870-71. This was followed, in the Punjab, by the Punjab Local Rates Act or Act XX of 1871. By this Act, the Local Government was empowered to charge, as from time to time might be deemed necessary, a rate on all land not exceeding six pies for every rupee of its annual value. The amount of annual value was to be considered as equivalent to double the land revenue assessed or assessable on any land.[1] In July 1873, further change was made in the financial arrangements of the province. A General Local Fund was formed. This included the local Rate, the Educational Cess, and other local revenues. After deducting certain charges (*e.g*, fixed contributions towards the cost of the Central Controlling establishments, the pay of hospital establishments)[2], the balance was to be distributed among districts in proportion. The cost of primary, female and middle vernacular schools situated in Municipalities was to be charged to the General Local Fund.[3] The cost of subordinate inspection was now transferred to Provincial services, but the charges on account of the items noted in the margin were to be paid from District Funds. The new arrangement while it provided for no fixed sum to be spent on education empowered the District Committees "to expend from District funds on educational purposes any sum beyond the actual assignment that they might be able to spare from the assignment made to them by Government for general purposes. "To sum the general effect of this Act,' as remarked by the Administation Report 1882-83," was in the course of the next few years to double the amount hitherto received from the education cess, and thus to increase largely the means at the disposal of the

1. Cost of Vernacular Schools other than those maintained in Municiyalties.

2. Grants-in-aid to the above and scholarships in the same.

3. Half cost of Normal Schools and the cost of stipends to village teachers studying in Normal Schools.

[1] See the Punjab Administration Report, 1871-72, pages 20-22.

[2] Punjab Administration Report 1872-73, paragraphs 146-155.

[3] Punjab Education Report, 1873-74.

new District Committees for the education of the agricultural class."

A few remarks about fees have now to be made. To begin with, no fees were levied in Government Schools, though under the grant-in-aid Rules, some fees were charged in private institutions of higher and middle classes. In Government Schools, it was proposed to levy small fees from the pupils attending Tahsil and Zillah schools as soon as they became thoroughly organized. The Supreme Government also recommended the charging of fees from boys of commercial and non-agricultural classes attending village Schools, because these classes contributed nothing for education, although the village schools, maintains from the education cess levied on zemindars only were equally open to them.[1] In 1860-61, fees were levied in Government Schools of all grades except Female Schools and Normal Schools The rate of fees charged was, however, very low, ranging from one to two annas per month in Tahsil and Village Schools and from one to four annas or eight annas in Zillah Schools. A certain amount was also levied in higher schools on the first admission of a boy. In the Government Colleges opened in 1864, the rate of tuition fees charged was two rupees per month. The funds available for Zillah schools were, however, very insufficient, as Government would not ordinarily allow more than Rs. 3,000 per annum per school and in 1866-67 the rate of fees was increased by one-half everywhere and in some cases doubled. The rate of fees then varied in Zillah Schools from four annas to two rupees, while fees in other institutions remained the same. Fees in Zillah Schools were further increased in 1869-70, from

[1] Punjab Records, January 1860.

four annas to twelve annas, and fixed at one rupee in 1876-77, where they remained stationary till the close of this period. It is needless to say that the possibility of the increased rate of fees in Zillah schools was in an index to the desire of the upper classes for English Education.

(3) *Grants-in-aid.*—The Despatch of 1854 set before the Indian Government the high ideal of the intellectual uplift of the whole mass of people, under its cars. The State was to provide the necessary organisation for inspection, advice, and encouragement and also to set up schools and colleges of its own. But it was impossible even if it were desirable that it should bear the entire cost of providing a sound education for a country so densely populated as India. The Chief aim of Government Schools aod Colleges was to set a standard and to create amongst the people a desire for the government system of education, and Government institutions were to be established and maintained only where people lacked the desire or ability to provide institutions of their own.

The period therefore opened very favourable for institutions under private management. These were to be aided and encouraged by Government by means of a system of grants-in-aid. No rivalry between these and Government Schools was to be suffered, indeed the latter were to be "restricted to those places at which there might be no effective schools under missionary superintendence or in which the ground might not have been otherwise preoccupied."[1] In pursuance of this policy Government Schools at Jullundur and Kangra were withdrawn, and it was olny as a special case that Govern-

[1] Punjab Records, March, 1855.

ment was persuaded to maintain Schools at Rawalpindi and Amritsar where Mission Schools also existed.[1] Finally, the charges of the Education Department were not to be increased indefinitely lest private bodies should find it impossible to complete with the public authorities and the Supreme Government actually suggested in the beginning of 1857, that some check was required on the expenses of the Education Department in the Punjab.[2]

Indigenous Schools in the Punjab, in accordance with the policy detailed above, were to be classified and fostered; they were to be "*aided* so that, thus partly supported by a system of Grants-in-Aid, they might become in some degree amenable to Government supervision and form the nucleus of a new, improved, and organised system.[3]

The main conditions to be fulfilled by Schools entitled to a Government grant were few and simple. The Schools were to be open to Government inspection;[4] grants were to be made only for secular education, there was to be absolutely no interference with religious instruction on the part or Inspecting Officers who were to take no notice of it; some fee, however small, was to be charged from pupils attending these schools;[5] grants were to be made, not for the general expenses of the school, but for specific purposes. *i. g.*, Salaries of the

---

[1] See Punjab Record, August, 1856.

[2] Punjab Records, January, 1857.

[3] Punjab Records, September, 1859.

[4] In the Punjab a small grant was however given to female schools not open to inspection by Government officers.

[5] Female Schools, purely Vernacular Schools, and Normal Schools were, however, exempted from this provision (Revised Grants-in-aid Rules, 1864-65).

Staff, Buildings, or Equipment, and lastly, the amount of State aid was not ordinarily to exceed one-half of the entire expenditure on an institution. The various aims of observing religious neutrality, stimulating private enterprise and aiding educational institutions were thus harmonised.

We have now to trace the effects and subsequent history of these measures. Rs. 720, per mensem were sanctioned by the Chief Commissioner, Punjab, in 1856, for affording aid to institutions of the higher class. The indigenous Schools were to be aided out of the yields of the one per cent cess. The higher and a few lower schools which were at that time all missionary institutions readily availed themselves of Government aid, Ten Schools were in receipt of aid by the close of the year.

The case of the indigenous Schools was, however, different. The teachers of these Schools while they readily accepted the aid proffered by Government entirely ignored the fulfilment of the conditions on which such aid was granted. No scheme of secular studies was introduced by them; there were no classes, but as before, "mere assemblages of lads." The scheme of making the existing indigenous Schools the nucleus of a new and improved system completely broke down and had soon to be given up as also the original promoters of these institutions attempted, when the prospect of Government aid was held out to these schools, to withhold their own contributions and to throw the whole burden of support on the Educational cess. The Education Department henceforth took no notice of these schools; they could not be improved and were to be generally replaced[1] by schools established

[1] See The History and Prospects of British Education in India, page 82.

by the Department, although the attitude of the Department to the former was by no means hostile. The government system gradually reacted on better schools of the class and in 1861-62, the teachers and pupils of an indigenous school solicited the Inspector to assist them in studying Arithmetic and Geography.[1] Gradually some of the schools were placed on the list of aided institutions. "The Managers of Arabic and Sanskrit Schools were religious studies were pursued were averse to accept grant-in-aid from Government but the Managers of Persian Schools (some of which were very good ones), seemed more inclined to accept Government aid and inspections."[2] A large number of indigenous schools, 468, were brought on the list of aided Institutions in 1867-77 and the number of such schools continued to show a slight increase during the following years.

The story of the indigenous Schools has carried us almost to the close of our period and we must now go back to consider the attitude of Government towards private enterprise in relation to higher and vernacular education, for the question of higher education presented no serious problem. This education which generally meant English Education was in demand for its value in terms of livelihood in the form of Government service[3] and because a knowledge of English as the language of the ruling class also offered the prospect of elevation of social rank and status. Besides, the system of grants-in-aid was welcomed in the Punjab by missionaries who were in possession of the field as promoters of the Government system of education.

---

[1] Punjab Administration Report, 1861-62.
[2] Punjab Administration Report, 1859-60.
[3] Lord Harding's Proclamation of 1844.

A different tale must be told of the experience gained with respect to elementary education. Local support required for the establishment of such schools under the grants-in-aid system was not forthcoming as the masses could not in the first place afford to pay subscriptions (freehold tenures for schools having been resumed by the Government), in addition to school-fees, and, secondly, because they did not yet properly understand the new Government system of education so as to appreciate its advantages and to be willing to pay for it. The experience in other Provinces was also the same and the matter was disposed of by the Secretary of State in his Despatch of 1859 which said "that the grant-in-aid system as hitherto in force, was unsuited to the supply of vernacular education to the masses of the population, and that the means of elementary education should be provided by the direct instrumentality of the officers of Government."[1] It may be remarked *en passant* that these instructions had been to some extent anticipated in this province where village Schools had been established on the *Halqa Bandi* system.[2]

The same despatch also announced an important modification of Government policy as regards the future of Government Schools and Colleges. The tenure of these, according to the Despatch of 1854, was clearly to be temporary: they were to be set up where no privately-managed institution existed but where the necessity and demand for education was real and generally felt; they were, however, to be withdrawn as soon as some private body either established schools or colleges of its own or was able and willing to administer

[1] Despatch of 1859, paragraph 50
[2] See Mr. Arnold's Report, 1856-57, paragraphs 52-58.

the institution owned and managed by Government who was then to make over the same to such private agency. The despatch of 1859, however, made no mention of the policy of closing Government institutions or of transferring them to the management of local bodies. Government institutions were to be increased where necessary, This was confirmed later by the Despatch of 23rd January, 1864. So Government was not to retire from the field although it would heartily welcome and substantially help private effort in the cause of education.

Judged by its results during this period, the system of grants-in-aid was on the whole a great success. While in 1859-60, the aid given by Government amounted only to Rs. 19,669 distributed among 20 institutions ; in1883-84 at the close of the period, there were 195 institutions in receipt of Rs.2,08,792. The expenditure from other sources during 1860-61, and 1883-84, was respectively Rs. 25,323 and Rs. 2,33,249. In other words, the expenditure of money on grants (1) meant more schools and more extensive education, (2) was instrumental in extracting out of the private means of the people an amount exceeding two lakhs and a quarter ; and (3) afforded the people valuable training in managing their own institutions and in learning to look after the educational needs of their community.

5

Second period—II

In the foregoing chapter we have dealt with general organisation and the financial aspect of the system of education introduced in the Punjab in accordance with the despatch of 1854. The various modifications that these underwent subsequently have also been duly considered. It, therefore, now remains for us to speak of the contribution made by these arrangements to the spread of education in the province.

(1) *Primary Education.*

As regards general education, we shall, while describing the various grades, employ the present-day classification of Primary Secondary, and College Education in preference to any archaic nomenclature, as our aim, in the study of the causation of events or movements, is to find out how the present is an outcome of the past and to narrate the story of the play of forces which have shaped the educational world of to-day.

The subject of Primary Education during this period divides itself into three well-marked sub-periods. The first period extense over seven years till the close of the year 1862. The institution imparting education generally up to this standard were the indigenous Schools, Village Schools, and Tahsil Schools. There were also a few aided Schools, ten or eleven, of the Lower Class under the Christian Missonaries. A detailed description of indigenous Schools has already been given.[1] The Villages Schools were established on the *Halqa-Bandi* System described in Chapter III (Page 22). The work of establishing these schools had already been in hand since January, 1855, when the Education Cess was authoritatively levied in the Province, and there were 170 one per cent. cess schools, with 2,550 children, in existence by January, 1856, when the Education Department was instituted. Akin to the Village Schools, but imparting an education of a less elementary character, there were the Tahsil Schools, maintained at first out of the general revenues, and situated at the headquarters of Tahsils.

(1) The instruction imparted in the Village Schools was of the most elimentary character, including the 3 Rs.' *i.e.*, reading and writing Urdu and elementary arithmetic, but it was well-adopted to the requirements of the people.[2] In the Tahsil Schools, the education consisted only of the rudiments of history, geography, airthmetic, and grammar. An important change was introduced in connection with these schools in 1862-63. Vernacular Schools were henceforth to be classified as Town Schools and Village Schools. The instruction in the two classes of institutions corresponded respectively to the middle and the primary standards. Consequent on this change, the former separation of Village Schools from

---

[1] See pages 36-37.

[2] Punjab Records, September, 1859.

Tahsil Schools was no longer necessary and the Tahsil Schools which did not fuifil the conditions prescribed for Town Schools were amalgamated with Village Schools. The new division was, however, not adopted uniformly in case of institutions under private management, some of which continued to be called by the one name of Schools of the lower class.

(2) This sub-period which lasted up to 1868 was also marked by another change of policy with regard to Primary or Village Schools. A popular Schools where attendance was very meagre were closed. Her causes of the decline of these Schools were the inefficiency of village school teachers (Rs. five per mensem being the pay for the lowest grade), and the want of proper supervision, because the Chief School Moharrir, the official employed in most districts for the purpose, was ill-paid, of low social standing, and very imperfectly educated. These remarks do not, however, apply to aided Private Schools in the case of which the number both of institutions and of scholars therein were on the increase.

The present-day classification of schools into High, Middle and Lower Class Schools was adopted in 1868-69.From 1871-72, the number of classes maintained in the Village was also reduced room eight to four, the first general examinations by the Upper and lower Primary Standards being held in 1872-73. In 1879-80, when the new system of classification for India was introduced, English schools were classed separately from Vernacular ones. The classification of schools obtaining from

1879-80 may be thus expressed in the from of a diagram :—

Schools for General Education.

- Secondary.
  - English.
    - Govern-ment.
    - Aided.
  - Vernacular.
    - Gevern-ment.
    - Aided.
- Primary.
  - English.
    - Govern-ment.
    - Aided.
  - Vernacular.
    - Govern-ment.
    - Aided.

Attention has been drawn to the inefficiency of teachers on account of the low standard of pay. The initial pay was raised, in 1869-70, from Rs. 5 to Rs. 10 and the maximum that might be reached was also increased from Rs. 12 to Rs. 20 per mensem. The condition of the Subordinate Inspecting Staff was, as already narrated, much improved by the measures sanctioned in 1876-77.

The former measure mentioned above had, however, an adverse effect upon the progress of eduction, which effect was further aggravated because expenditure on these schools from the education cess exceeded the income from that fund. Schools had to be closed to keep the expenditure within the limits of the income and during the next few years the number of village schools fell from 1129 to 1042 schools. But the decentralization of finance in 1871 and the financial measures of 1872-73, narrated elsewhere, soon saved the situation ; the eleven years which follewod were a period of continuous progress, till in 1883-84, the number of Government Primary Schools stood at 1403 schools with 97, 195 scholars, while 9,742 boys were receiving education in the 126 Aided Schools (including seven schools for boys of European or Eurasian parentage) of the same class. As regards the state of education in various areas, "the Hoshiarpur District was said to be the best in the province. But in the hill districts, on the Trans-Indus Frontier, and in the Multan and Hissar Divisions, education was not valued by the masses and the only good schools were in the towns."[1]

(2) *Secondary Education.*

The various stages by which demarcation between Schools of Primary and Secondary Grades was gradually brought about have already been narrated in the previous section. We shall, therefore, now mention a few other points of importance in connection with the High and Middle School Education.

The Zillah or Anglo-Vernacular Schools established by the District Officers during the previous period, were, including Schools at Sialkot and Ferozepore founded in 1855, of two classes, *viz.*, Superior Schools in which the medium of instruction was chiefly English, and inferior Schools in which the Vernacular formed the medium. The education imparted was a "training of faculties rather than a moral training, or a regulation of habits."[2]

The directions about the medium of instruction, contained in the despatch of 1854, have already been noticed (See page 26). The Zillah Schools established by the Department stood in the same relation to the Tahsil schools as the latter did to the Village schools. The curriculum of Zillah schools comprised the Vernacular studies prescribed for Tahsil schools, but on a higher scale, and it embraced a greater variety of subjects. English classes were also to be formed for the instruction of

---

[1] Punjab Administration Report, 1882-83.

[2] Punjab Administration Report, 1849-50, 50-51, on Amritsar School.

of those pupils who might be desirous of learning the English language.

The incorporation of the Calcutta University in 1857 led also in the Punjab to the gradual differentiation of schools imparting Collegiate education or education up to the level of the Entrance Examination of the said University, from those which, though situated at headquarters, did not reach that standard. A scheme of studies for Zillah schools revised on the basis of the requirements of the said Entrance Examination was issued in 1860-61 and students from the Punjab began to appear at the Entrance Examination of the Calcutta University from the next year, when there were three schools, at Lahore, Amritsar, and Delhi, teaching up to that standard. The distinction between these two grades of schools was clearly recognised in 1868-69, when the Zillah High Schools were classed separately from seventeen Zillah middle schools where the instruction imparted did not reach the University standard. The former had three departments ; the Upper school containing the 9th, 8th, 7th Classes (nomenclature of classes adopted in 1871-72), the middle school containing the 6th, 5th, 4th and 3rd classes, and the lower school containing three classes (two classes from 1871-72). The number of aided Schools which sent up candidates for the Entrance Examination of the Calcutta and Punjab Universities (a narrative of the latter will be given elsewhere) was nine during the same year. By 1883-84, 2,030 candidates had matriculated from the various institutions in the Punjab. The hostels attached to schools date from 1869-70.

The middle Schools comprised, in addition to the middle departments which formed a part of the High Schools, Zillah

Schools of middle class and Town Schools instituted in 1862-63. The Zillah middle Schools usually maintained only the four classes of the Middle Department, though the three classes of the Lower Schools were attached to some of them. In the Town schools there were eight classes, but the number of classes was reduced to six in consequence of the measures adopted in 1871-72. The District Schools, usually located at District headquarters, were for the benefit of the District at large ; they were under the direct management of the Department and were maintained at the expense of Government. The Town schools comprised schools under Deputy Commissioners and Cantonment schools. Vernaculars chools, under Deputy Commissioners, were maintained almost entirely by funds out of local sources, while other schools received some grant from Government. In the district schools, English formed a subject of study from the lowest class, while the course in Town schools was purely vernacular, though provision for the study of English existed in most schools. The number of Government English and Government Vernacular Middle Schools in 1883-84 was 44 and 128, respectively, or 172 schools in all, as compare with 90 institutions (20) zillah schools imparting education belowthe Entrance Examination Standard and 70 Town Schools) in 1864-65. The number of aided institutions under private management included, by the close of 1883-84, eight Secondary Schools for Europeans and Eurasians and 32 for Natives.

The Middle School Examination was instituted by the Department in 1869-70. The Middle School Examination for Europeans and Eurasians was, however, not held till 1880-81, and the conduct of the former was also transferred to the Punjab University in 1883-84.

In as much as Primary schools were finally separated from Secondary schools in 1869-80, the progress as to the number of scholars can only be estimated by comparing the following figures for the same year with those for 1883-84.[1]

	Government English Secondary Schools.	Government Vernacular Secondary Schools.	Aided Secondary Schools	Aided Vernacular Secondary Schools
1879-80 ..	2,437	2,495	1,171	..
1883-84 ..	3,289	3,307	1,393	..

It must be admitted that a comparison extending only over four years cannot be conclusive. Some idea of the progress made during this period may, however, be obtained, if we compare the above-mentioned figures for 1883-84 with those for Government schools on Ist January, 1856.[2] There were on that date 1,764 scholars in the eighteen Government schools in existence, while the average number of scholars receiving Secondary Education in Government Schools in 1883-84 amounted to 6,596, which meant an increase of 4,832 scholars. When it is further considered that during this period the Department established a high school at almost every District headquarters, about two Anglo-Vernacular Middle schools in every district, and 128 Vernacular Middle Schools for mass education, its present achievement and

1 Punjab Administration Report, 1883-84.

2 Mr. Arnold's Report for 1856-57, paragraph 88.

future programme may be summed up in the remark that while an educational standard had been attained and a sufficient number of schools to show the way had also been established, craving for knowledge had yet to be created in the Punjab so that the existing schools might be still better attended and more schools opened by Government or the people themselves.

The expenditure incurred by Government from all sources on Secondary schools where about 8,000 pupils were receiving education was in 1883-84, Rs. 2,73,338 ; while that on Primary Education (including the Normal schools for teachers for Primary schools) was for the same year Rs. 4,65,106 on about 1,00,000 scholars in Primary Schools. The Primary Schools were designed to serve the bulk of the population, while only a select few availed themselves of the Middle and High Schools. The distribution of expenditure on the education of masses and of advanced classes which constituted respectively 90 per cent and 10 per cent of the entire population was, even if we take into consideration the fact that the Secondary education must naturally be more expensive than the Elementary education, palpably disproportionate, being roughly in the ratio of 1·75:1. The importance of the uplift of the masses as contrasted with the advancement of the few upper classes cannot be over-rated and the former evidently deserved greater attention and more substantial help on the part of Government than it had hitherto received.

(3) Colleges and The Punjab University.

The despatch of 1854 had sanctioned the establishment of Colleges for general and special education in the various provinces. In the Punjab, hhowever, it was considered advisable to postpone the establishment of a College at Lahore until students to avail of it were forthcoming.

As already stated, students from Punjab schools began to appear at the Entrance Examination of the Calcutta University from 1861-62, and thirteen candidates had matriculated by the close of the year 1862-63. A first class Government High School at Lahore, had already been started in 1859-60 in partial compliance with the express request of the Sirdars of the province for the founding of a College; and a Government College at Lahore was established on 1st January, 1864. Another Government College was also opened the same year at Delhi, which possessed before the Mutiny a College imparting a fair English and the highest order of Oriental education (*i.e.*, Arabic, Persian, and Urdu) The authorities of the St. Stephen's School, Delhi, also started two College Classes but were soon persuaded to send the matriculated students of their school to the Government College at Delhi. College Classes were also attached to the Lahore Mission School from the same year, *viz.*, 1864-65, but had to be closed in December, 1869, as there was no room for two colleges at Lahore. It is to be noted that though Natural Science was one of the subjects of study from 1877-78, there was no provision for a scheme of studies on the basis of a Science Faculty and all the candidates appeared in Examinations on the Arts side.

The colleges were not well attended because students could not afford to pay the cost of books and to defray the charges for their maintenance Stipends, varying from Rs. ten to Rs. seventeen per mensem at the Lahore College and Rs. ten to Rs. twenty-eight at the Delhi College, were given by Government which, according to the rules issued by the Government of India, provided a Government scholarship for one student out of every four who had passed the Calcutta Universty Examination. The Punjab University College, sanctioned in 1868-69, also devoted Rs. 8,400 per annum to scholarships to be held by the students of the two Government Colleges, so that every student was in receipt of a scholarship of some kind. Even these liberal measures did not succeed in keeping students at College who often could not resist the temptation of Government service so easily available in those days and left college without cempleting their education.

The cost of the maintenance of Colleges was, therefore, very high, being,during 1872-73, Rs. 70,551 for the education of 84 scholars attending the two Colleges. An indirect consequence both the Colleges had to be inadeqately staffed for want of funds.

In view of the above circumstances, the Government College at Delhi was, in 1876-77, abolished or amalgamated with the Lahore Government College which was soon provided with an excellent staff and where improvement was visible from year to year so that, in 1883-84, there were 129 students on the rolls, with an average daily attendance of 115 scholars. Scholarhips too were not now so essential to a collegiate education as forty-one per cent of the students were without scholarships; and the time had come when the number of Government Scholarships could be fixed irrespective of the number of passes.

A College at Delhi had also been again started. In 1882-83, St. Stephen's college, maintained by the Cambridge Mission, was brought under the grant-in-aid system and twenty-three scholars were receiving education there in 1883-84.

We shall now speak of the Punjab University. The establishment of a University in the Punjab was not a part of the official educational programme, as there was yet no demand for it and as the despatch of 1854 had also recommended the immediate establishment of Universities only at the three presidency towns.

Dr. Leither, the first Principal of the Lahore Government College, was a scholar of Arabic and Turkish and as such he was naturally interested in the promotion of Oriental learning. A study of the educational system in vogue in the Province gave him the impression that the system of tuition as pursued in Government College and at the Calcutta University was not helpful to the progress of Oriental learning and as such unsuited to the needs of the Province.[1] A society, known as the Anjuman-i-Punjab, was founded under his auspices in 1865 and a proposal for a University was formulated the same year. The aim of the proposal was to give a new character to the general education of the people and to found a University with special and separate institutions throughout the country for attaining this purpose, quite independent of the Government system.

The proposal was duly considered by Government, and the Director of Public Instruction, in his letter of 9th January, 1868, also endorsed the view that the effect of the Calcutta University was unhealthy upon Vernacular and even English education as pursued in Zillah Schools and Government Colleges.

The result was a sort of compromise. The Supreme Government signified its general approval to the principles of the

---

[1] Resolution of Punjab Government on Educational Report for 1 865-66, paragraph 4.

movement, but was of opinion that the establishment of a University for the Punjab was premature. It, therefore, only sanctioned the establishment of an aided institution to be stayled the "Punjab University College," which might be expanded into a University hereafter.

The Punjab University College was started in 1869-70 and its special aims were to be—

(*a*) to promote the diffiusion of European Sciences, as far as possible, through ths medium of the Vernacular languages of the Punjab, and tht improvement and extension of Vernacular literature generally ;

(*b*) to associate the learned and influential Classes in the promotion and supervision of popular education.

The year 1869-70 was a very busy period for the Punjab University College. A Senate of 70 members was appointed by the Lieuterant Governor. Rules for the conduct of examinations and the grant of Certificates of proficiency were passed by the Senate. Scholarships were assigned to the Lahore and Delhi Colleges. A Sanskrit Professor and a Law Lecturer were appointed. The Lahore Medical School was affiliated and Faculties of Law Arts Medicine, and Engineering were formed. An Entrance Examination was prescribed and special examinations in Arbic, Sanskrit, and Persian were instituted. Lastly, an Oriental School (which gradually developed into an Oriental College) was established for enabling those who had made eome progress in Arabic and Sanskrit to perfect themselves in these languages.

From 1871-72, students had the choice of appearing either at the Examinations of the Calcutta University or those of the

Punjab University Colleges. Most of them appeared at both, at the former in order to receive the stamp which the University is supposed to impress and eventually to secure the University Degree; at the latter so that they might be entitled to the scholarships granted by the University College The system of College scholarships, stipends, prizes National scholarships, and patronage of literature soon won the University College the popularity it deserved ; the number of candidates appearing at its Entrance, Proficiency, and High Proficiency Examinations steadily increased, while the number of those appearing at the corresponding Examinations, Entrance First Arts, and B. A. Examinations of the Calcutta University, decreased in proportion. Besides, the Punjab University College also held examinations in Oriental learning, Sanskrit, Arabic, and Persian Shastri, Maulvi Fazil, or Munshi Alim.

The Punjab University College had therefore amply fulfilled the hopes raised by its establishment and the aspirations of the promoters of a University in the Punjab were realised at last when "the Secretary of State, on being satisfied that the examinations of the Punjab University College were of such a nature as to justify that body being entrusted with the power to grant degrees, accorded his permission to the introduction of an Act for the incorporation of a University in 1888.[1]" By the Act of 1882, the Punjab University was incorporated on the model of the London University, like the sister Universities established at Presidency towns, and received the power of conferring degrees for Oriental Learning and Arts. The power to confer degrees in Law, Medicine, Science, and Engineering was to be granted by Governor-General when the arrangements and examinations were such as to render the

[1]Punjab Administration Report, 1882-83, paragraph 826.

grant of these powers desirable.

The usefulness of the Punjab University continued to grow in the following year, the closing year of our period, when it was declared that "it had almost driven its sister of Calcutta out of the field as regards natives of the province, while the considerable number of candidates who appeared for its examinations in Oriental languages from institutions beyond the limits of the Punjab showed that it was also appreciated further afield.[1]

We may close this section with a mention of the number of candidates who had passed the various examinations on the Arts side of both the Calcutta University and the Punjab University College of the Punjab University up to 1883-84 Briefly stated the statistics for the period stood as below :—

Examinations.		*Passes.*
First Arts or Proficiency in Arts ...	English ...	352
Intermediate	Oriental ...	8
B. A. or High Proficiency in Arts...	English ...	95
B. O. L.	Oriental ...	4
M. A. or Honours in Arts ...	English ...	26
M. C. L.	Oriental ...	3

To sum up, About 500 candidates in all had received an education of a higher order in European sciences by the close of the period, and we may say that a statisfactory beginning in the direction of advanced learning had certainly been made; especially in its University, the Punjab had secured the sure means of progress in Oriental as well at English education.

[1]Punjab Administration Report, 1883-84, paragraph 826.

5

Second Period—III

We have so far noticed the working of the present educational system and traced the progress and development of mass as well as higher education in this province. In this chapter we shall treat of female education, vocational training, etc., emboided in the comprehensive measure of 1854, and discribe also the auxiliary means that were adopted for, or spontaneously arose to help, the diffusion of education in the widest sense of the term.

I.—*Female Education.*

To deal fist with female education the supreme importanc of women for the well-being of a country can hardly be overated, as all efforts concentrated merely upon male education can but lead to poor results in the case of intellectual, motal, and social uplift of its people as long as the females remain steeped in ignorance. The Educational despatch of 1854 had commended the subject of Female Education to the care of the Supreme Government and the matter recieved due attention at the hands of the local Government all over India. It was yet in this sphere that the educational efforts of the Punjab Education Department met with the greatest discouragement and the problem down to the close of the period appeared, if not absolutely insoluble, really elusive and highly perplexing.

The reasons for this state of things are not far to seek. In the case of boys, secular education, though not sharply distinguished from religious instruction, was not a new thing to the Punjab. The task of introducing western education among the boys, though not without its difficulties, was consequently not so uphill, and the decision to replace and absorb indigenous Schools which refused to reform themselves was soon made. The conception of the Punjabi as regards Female Education was, however, radically different from the Western Ideal. As stated elsewhere the home was considered to be the natural and the only proper place for woman and religion constituted not only the most potent but perhaps the exclusive influence in her education. The conceptiou of Hindu marriages as a sacrament for the fulfilment ef religious duties is an illustrations in point. The sort of Female education which a Punjabi might have welcomed cou'd only be one which gave woman no taste for anything outside her home and no interest in any man except her husband; and the education offered by Government which was much like boy's education, which might break the traditional bonds and lead to women aspiring for service in public offices private shops and firms or for the membership of municipalities or councils, as in the case of European women, was naturally looked upon with uneasiness, if not abhorrence.

Besides these fundamental differences, there were less important, though real, difficulties which retarded the progress of Female Education in the Punjab. As instances, we may mention the custom of marriage at an early age among the Hindus and the purdah system among the Muslims and a section of Hindu society, which latter manifested itself in the objection against the inspection of schools by male officers of the Government.

Under these circumstances it is not surprising, if no substantial results were achieved during the quarter of century under review. The time and money spent in this cause did not, however, go in vain ; popular prejudices were gradually removed, the interest and co-operation of the native community was secured, and measures for putting native female education upon a more satisfactory basis could be introduced at the close of the period with perhaps a greater chance of success.

The above remarks do not of course apply to Euorpeans and Eurasians of the Indian Christians in the Punjab. An adequate number of schools chiefly under missionary control were maintained for their requirements, and all these were under the grant-in-aid system.

The work of the Department in this direction may now be briefly summarised. Seventeen female schools were opened during 1856-57, the first year of the existence of the department. Most of these had soon to be closed for want of scholars, though a large number of schools were opened in Jullundur District under the fostering care of Captain Elphinstone, the Deputy Commissioner. The number of the female schools in the Punjab was, at the close of 1861-62, fifty-two primary schools with 1,312 scholars who were supposed to be able to decipher the alphabet, besides reading or repeating their religious books.

In 1862-63, in an Educational Durbar, the Leiutenant Governor addressed the Chiefs of Lahore and Amritsar on the need for attention to this important subject The response made to this appeal was indeed splendid. Family priests were to be appointed on a salary to teach girls by going from house to house and these girls as they became efficient were to be employed as governesses. The increase in the number of schools established by Government and by private bodies or individuals—Baba Khem Singh being one of the most zealous among individual workers—was indeed phenomenal, till by 1865-66, the number of Government and Aided Schools had risen to 333 and 696 schools, respectively, with 6,834 and 12,727 pupils on the rolls. The instruction imparted was not satisfactory, but it was believed that popular prejudices were being removed.

The reaction soon set in, however, and schools had to be gradually closed on account of dearth of teachers, very poor attendance, or miserably inefficient instruction which brought education into disrepute. The number of institutions, both Government and aided, decreased continually, till in 1878-79 the figures stood at only 195 Government and 232 aided primary schools. Of the latter, sixty-two were Mission schools which were generally doing better work than others, whether aided or Govornment.

The schools at Lahore and Amritsar, however, fared much better. Trained English mistresses held charge of most schools, an inspectress of schools was appointed, and arrangements were made in 1868-69 for allowing married scholars to continue their studies.

In 1883-84, the close of this period, 9,605 pupils were

receiving instruction in the 315 primary schools in the province, and twelve scholars were attending the three middle schools. As to aided school for European and Anglo-Indian girls, there were ten primary schools with 679 scholars and three middle schools with nineteen scholars. The net cost to Government from general revenues amounted to Rs. 50,951 for all schools.

2. *Training of Teachers.*— One of the important characteristics which distinguished the British from the Indian system of education was, as already mentioned elsewhere, the recognition of the need for training or apprenticeship in the art of teaching. The opening of Normal schools had, therefore, already been contemplated by the educational scheme framed in 1854, so that the injunctions, contained on the subject in the Directors' despatch of the same year, were simply instrumental in accelerating the progress of work in this direction.

As to the training of teachers for Primary schools, Normal schools were opened at Lahore and Rawalpindi in 1856 and 1857. The school at Delhi followed next year and five more schools had been opened at various places by the close of 1859-60. These five schools were subsequently amalgamated with the schools at Lahore, Rawalpindi, and Delhi, as it was considered more desirable to have a few first class institutions serving the various parts of the Province than a large number of institutions scattered about at unimportant places where educational facilities might not be easily available. The number of Government Normal schools therefore, stood at three from 1869-70 to the close of this period. In addition to these there existed at Amritsar an aided Normal school which had been opened in 1866-67 by the Christian Vernacular Educational Society working at the place. In 1883-84,

174 scholars were in attendance at the three Government Normal schools, while the numder of pupils studying in the aided school was 32. The initial period of training was six months though most of the teachers were called up again after two or three years to undergo fresh training for about a year. By 1864-65, most of the teachers had received training at these schools and the time of training was then extended, till it covered a period of three years.

Most of the candidates sent for training, at these schools were men of miserably poor education, and the instruction imparted at the Normal schools was consequently of the nature of general education, very little time being available for professional training, though Model Primary schools for practice of teaching were attached to these schools. No improvement in the quality of candidates could however, be expected so long as the average village school teacher received only a pittance of Rs.five per mensem, and the amount of stipend allowed to pupil-teachers was as low as Rs. three per mensem.

As alredy described, the measures of 1869-70, improved the prospects of village teachers to some extent and the Middle School Examination was also instituted the same year. A change in the system of selection of candidates for Normal school, was consequently introduced. Boys who passed the Middle School Examination were to be engaged as pupil-teachers and eventually sent up for training at the Normal Schools. The system of examination was also modified in 1872-73. At the end of two years' study, an examination was to be held for the Primary Teachers' Certificate. The third year of study was to be optional and the examinations held thereafter qualified the candidate to teach in a Middle

School. In a word, using the present day terminology, a differentiation was henceforth to be made between teachers holding Junior-Vernacular and those holding Senior Vernacular Certificates.

The training of female teachers was during this period left entirely to private enterprise. The first Normal School for native mistresses was opened at Delhi by the S.P.G. Mission in 1863-64. Normal Schools were next year opened at Lahore and Amritsar by the Committee for promoting female education and schools at other places followed shortly after. The European Training School at Delhi was established in 1875-76. In 1883-84, the number of Female aided Normal schools stood at six schools for Indians and one school for Europeans, containing 187 and four pupils respectivley. The condition of these schools, excepting the Amritsar Schools, was however far from satisfactory ; the standard of education was very low and it was generally felt that the system of separate Normal Schools for Indian girls had failed. A number of Christian ladies, English and Indian, working under the zenana missions instituted in 1855, also imparted some secular instruction to Hindu ladies in their homes.

Mention has been made of the measures of 1872-73 which provided for the training of vernacular teachers for Middle schools. The need for the training of English teachers was recognised as early as 1859[1], but the necessary provision was not made before 1880-81 when the Central Training College was established to prepare English and Vernacular teachers for Secondary Schools. The English Class consisted of students

[1] Punjab Records, September 1859 : letter from the Director of Public Instruction to the Financial Commissioner.

admitted from the Lahore College and promising teachers sent up for training. Eleven scholars were on the rolls in the first year. The Vernacular Class which consisted of third year students shifted from Normal schools, contained thirty-five scholars. A lower class for training English Teachers for the Upper Primary Department of English Schools was formed two years later, so that before our period closed, the Central Training College contained the Senior Anglo-Vernacular and Junior Anglo-Vernacular Classes for English teachers and the Senior Vernacular Class for Vernacular teachers The manifold activities of the College do not fall within the scope of this work but it is of interest to know that the genesis of the scheme of school gardens which form a feature of most of the schools to-day may be traced back to the earliest days of the college, whose Principal, Mr. Dick, had a passion for garden work.

3. *Special Education.*— We now proceed to describe briefly the state of special education under which head are included Jail schools, Industrial schools, Professional Education, Education of special classes or sections, *viz.*, European and Anglo-Indian, Mohammadans, and Indian Chiefs ; and Missionary or charitable education.

1. *Jail Schools.*—Attention to the improvement of instruction imparted to prisoners was first given in 1862-63 when at the suggestion of the Director of Public Instruction trained teachers with best educated prisoners as pupil-teachers began to be employed in teaching the priscners in the various wards of the Lahore Central Jail. Next year the administration of Jail Schools was vested in the Education Department, though they were to be maintained cut of funds at the disposal of

the Inspector-General of Prisons. In 1863-64 there were twenty-three Jail Schools at work with 6,106 prisoners up to the age of 40. The age limit of prisoners to be instructed wa reduced to 25 years in 1877-78 when there were twenty-nine schools with 2,201 scholars. Urdu was taught most exclusively, but provision existed also for Nagri in the Ambala Circle Jail, English was to be restricted to those prisoners at the Lahore Central Jail, who were entered for very long terms, or for life, and who were therefore, trained to carry on the work of the government press. These were also trained as compositors. The administration of Jail Schools was taken over by the Prison authorities in 1878-79, and instruction, from the next year, was confined to three Jails, at Ludhiana, Multan, and Dera Ismail Khan, and at the female penitentiary at Lahore.

2. *Industrial Schools*.—The Mayo School of Art was established by Government in 1875-76. Its aim was instruction in drawing and designing rather than in mechanical work, though some attention was given to the latter in accordance with the wishes of the first promoters of the school and the actual necessities of the craftsmen of the province were not neglected. The Exhibition of Arts and manufactures held in its grounds in 1881-82, was a great success and gave some impetus to the institution which was in quite a flourishing condition at the close of our period, with sixty two scholars on the rolls.

Besides this school, there were four industrial schools for males and one school at Delhi for females The former included the school attached to the Horticultural Society garden. The male schools imparted instruction in carpentry, carpet-making, weaving, saddlery, and metal work. The females received instruction in lace work and embroidery.

3. *Professional Education.*—The Medical School, Lahore, was established by Government in 1860 to satisfy the demand for Punjabi doctors, as doctors from Bengal generally disliked taking up service so far from their homes and, when appointed, did not often command the confidence of the people. There were two Departments in the School, the class for Sub-Assistant Surgeons (known subsequently when the school was affiliated to the Punjab University College as Licentiate in Medicine and Surgery), and the class for Hospital Assistants and Doctors. Instructions in the Sub-Assistant Surgeon Class was in English and the course extended over five years. The Hospitals Assistants and Doctors received instruction in Urdu and the period of their instruction was three years. In 1879-80, an English Class for Hospital Assistants was also started. By 1883-84, the school had turned out 111 Sub-Assistant Surgeons or Licentiates in Medicine and Surgery and 384 Doctors and Hospital Assistants including 33 Hospital Assistants of the English Class instituted in 1879-80. It may be mentioned that the Licentiates in Medicine and Surgery and the English Class Hospital Assistants of those days are respectively the Assistant and Sub-Assistant Surgeons of to-day.

Attached to the Medical School were the Midwifery Class started in 1877-78 and the Practising Hakim Class added next year.

Besides the Medical Schools, there existed the Law School maintained by the Punjab University. The Veterinary College was not established till after the close of this period. Mensuration and Survey Classes also existed in certain schools from 1872-73 onwards, in order to develop a taste for engineering and provide students from the Roorki College.

4. *Education of Europeans and Anglo-Indians.*—This was the object of special attention by Government from 1871-72 onward and the Education Department also noticed separately in its annual report the state of arrangements existing for the education of Europeans and Anglo-Indians residing in the Punjab. The Resolution No. 8, dated the 8th October, 1881, of the Government of India also called upon the Local Governments to make further provision for the education of Europeans. The number of aided schools for their education rose from 9 in 1872 to 36 in 1883-84, and the aid rendered by Government from Rs. 22,095 to Rs. 63,239. The Lawrence Asylum at Sanawar was a Government institution under the Military Department. The inspection of these schools was, as mentioned in an earlier section, entrusted to the Inspector of Schools, Lahore Circle, in 1883-84, and the European Code for the Bengal Presidency was brought into force next year. The details of scholars attending these schools have already been given in their proper places, and it may be said that, by the close of our period, "the European and Anglo-Indians population of the Punjab was well-provided for in the matter of schools."[1]

5. *Education of Mohammadans.*— Special Attention to the education of Mohammadans was an all-India rather than a Punjab question. The attitude of Mohammadans towards the British system of Education had been unfriendly for a long time and the consequently backward condition of their education received for the first time the attention of Lord Mayo who,

[1] Punjab Administration Report, 1883-84.

in his Resolution, dated 7th August, 1871, invited the attention of the vorious Local Governments to the subject. Enquiries made in the Punjab, revealed, however, that the whole course of Primary Education was so shaped as to favour the Mohammadan equally with the Hindu and although the backwardness of Mohammadans was remarkable in the High Schools and in the Colleges, yet the existing system of State instruction as at least as favourable to Mohammadans as to Hindus. No special educational privileges to their community were therefore, needed in this province. The real causes of their backwardness in attendance at schools in the Punjab lay in their chiefly pursuing agricultural occupations and in their preponderance in the backward areas of the Derajat and Peshawar Divisions where Mohammadans formed 90 per cent of the population. Attendance of Mohammadan scholars continued to improve at institutions of all grades, till the percentage of Mohammadans attending educational institutions stood at 38·2 in 1882-83 compared with 34·9 in 1871-72 and the neglect of higher education on their part was also considered to be on the wane.

6. *Education of Indian Chiefs.*—No separate institutions for the purpose were establised by the Department during this period, though special classes were formed, from time to time, at the Lahore Government School. In 1859-60, there was a class at this school exclusively for the sons of the Chiefs and in 1871-72, a special class, known as the Sirdars' Class was formed of Lahore. The only special institution for the purpose was the Wards School at Ambala, established in 1867, primarily intended for the edudation of the Wards of Court of Ambala district, though sons of other gentlemen of rank were also admitted. The students received a liberal education in English

and the Vernacular, and were also taught riding and a variety of other exercises. But the number in attendance rarely exceeded a dozen and at the close of our period, a proposal was under consideration to replace it by a Punjab Chief's School at Lahore, which should be "a sort of Punjab Eton, to which boys of good family shou'd be admitted. and where the education should be thorough and fees high."[1]

7. *Missionary and Charitable Education.*—The pioneering activities of missionary bodies in the field of education were narrated in detail in a previous chapter Their efforts for this cause, although undertaken only as a means to the achievement of the evangelical missicn which they had primarily in view, continued unabated, and during this period there was a large increase in the number of institutions of all grades under their managment. These were, as a rule, first-class institutions; they were generally superior to schools established either by Government or other private bodies. The education of Europeans and Anglo-Indians was almost entirely in their hands and any attempts at educating the depressed classes were yet confined solely to them. The various institutions have been duly noticed in their proper places and what need be pointed out here is, that the debt this land owes to the missionaries working for its uplift is very great indeed.

IV.—*Accessory Measures and External agencies.*—We have so far described the progress of education during the longest and the most important period of our narrative and a brief mention of the chief accessory measures adopted to ensure the success of the educational system detalied in the foregoing pages, and of the agencies due to and working for the growth of educa-

[1] See the Punjab Administration Report, 1884-85.

tion in the province, may fitly close this review. In this section we shall speak of scholarships and stipends, the Government Book Depot and the Text-Book Committee, employment of students in the Public Service, the Central Museum, Lahore, the Press and Literature, Public Libraries, and Literary Societies.

1. *Scholarships and Stipends.*—Mention has already been made of the stipends given to Normal School student and of the scholarships and stipends granted by Government and the Punjab University to students at Government Colleges. Scholarhips were also held by scholars studying in the Central Training College, the Mayo School of Art, and the Medical School.

School scholarships ranging between rupees five and annas eight per mensem were at first tenable only in Government zillah Schools and the expenditure under this head stood at Rs. 209 per mensem. Open scholarships of the value of rupees eight to rupees three per mensem to be competed for by boys of inferior zillah or town schools were also provided in 1863-64, and boys of aided schools could avail themselves of them from the following year. Soon after the Middle School examination had been instuted, the award of scholarships was generally determiend by the position gained by the boys at this examination. Besides these scholarships from General revenues, scholarships not exceedig rupees three per mensem were granted by District Committees and Muncipalities. These were tenable in District and Vernacular schools of the Middle Class. In other words, scholarships granted by Government or Local Bodies were not tenable in any institutions but those under Government control. Scholarships were made tenable in aided Institutions from 1879-80. In 1882-83 the Government allotment for scholarships at both Government and aided High Schools was Rs. 18,000 for the year. A revised scheme for the award of College scholarsships granted by the University was also drawn up the same years. The system of the award of Government scholarships was radically changed in the closing year of our period when the number of both College and School Scholarships was fixed and the latter were distributed among districts and divisions, and all scholarships made tenable in aided as well as Government institutions.

2. *Government Book Depot and The Text-Book Committee.*—A Book and Translation Department was established in the beginning of 1857 for the supply to books needed for schools. The Depot was to work under the Director to whom Rs 10,000, were advanced by the Government for this purpose. An Educational Press was also maintained for lithographing the *Sarkari Akhbar* and Varnacular educational books. Books to the value of Rs. 3,000 were sold in the first year. The Depot became self-supporting in the course of a few years and was working at a profit from 1876-77. By 1882-83, the value of books issued had risen to Rs. 78,833. The monopoly, however, of the Depost for the supply of books to schools was now subject to, and the Depot was finally abolished in 1883-84 when much of the press work was also transferred to private firms.

The Text-Book Committee was first appointed in 1877 for the purpose of considering what English books should be recommended for the use of schools and colleges and supplied to the libraries of Government educational institutions. The Committee was reconstituted in 1881-82 and was empowered to deal with both English and Vernacular books. The new Committee held its first meeting in April, 1882, and by means of its various Sub-Committees, it soon surveyed the whole range of educational literature.

3. *Public Services and Education.*—Refernce has already been made to Lord Hrrdinge's proclamation of 1844 which held but a prospect of employment in the public service to those who had received an English education. In the Punjab, the proposal for prescribing educational tests for employment was approved by the Lieutenant Governor in 1864-65 and from 1875-76 official appointments and promotions were reserved for those who had passed the Middle School Examination. The tendency of College students to quit College for Government service has already been noticed. In 1882-83, the initial salaries of men of College education varied from Rs. 20 to Rs. 200 per mensem and students from Vernacular Middle Schools obtained service on an average salary of Rs. 8-6-0 per mensem and so there was on the whole no dearth of employment for young men of fair education, English or Vernacular.

4. *Central Muscum, Lahore.*—This was established by Government in 1865-66 and gained an ever-increasing popularity from year to year. Connection with the South-Kensington Museum was also established in 1880-81. By 1884, it contained the Coin-Department, Fine Arts Branch, and Stuffed Birds. Agricultural models were added in 1884-85 and several presentations of importance were made by private persons. The number of visitors had risen from 27,390 persons during 1869 to 2,51,003 persons in 1884.

5. *The Press and Literature.*— The censorship on the Vernacular Press imposed after the Mutiny was removed in 1865-66

and licenses were no longer necessary for the establishment of printing presses. The number of presses in the Province consequently increased to 42, as compared with 30 Presses in the previous year and eight vernacular newspapers were published in 1865-66 as compared with two the year before. The number of Vernacular books published was 167. By 1882-83, the number of presses had risen to 104. Seven English Newspapers and 28 Vernacular Newspapers were published besides seven English and 23 Vernacular Periodicals, and the number of publications registered under Act XXV of 1867, stood at 1,198 of which 858 were in Vernacular languages and 145 in Indian Classical languages. The taste for literature was being gradually developed, although works of permanent value yet bore only an insignificant proportion to the total number printed. The English Newspapers included the Indian Public Opinion (triweekly), the Moffusilite (bi-weekly), and the Civil and Military Gazette (weekly), which three papers were amalgamated into a single daily paper, the Civil and Military Gazette in 1876-77. The Indian Tribune also began to appear as a weekly paper from 1880. The Vernacular papers, except the Akhbar-i-Am, a bi-weekly paper, had yet a limited circulation; and most of them gave news only, rarely publishing original articles.

6. *Public Libraries.*—Complete information as to the public libraries existing in the Punjab was first obtained by the authorities in the beginning of 1857. No libraries were then maintained by Government. There existed several book-clubs at Lahore, Amritsar, and Sialkot maintained by private subscriptions. There was also a public library at Peshawar. Flourishing libraries existed also at Ambala Cantonment,

Ferozepore, and Simla. Most of these libraries were established after 1850. Not much was done in this direction during this period, as a reading public to make use of such libraries had not yet been created. The concluding year saw, however, the establishment of the Punjab Public Library at Lahore, which has grown to be one of the most important institutions of its kind in India.

7. *Literary Societies.*—A fairly complete census of these was obtained in 1882-83. The oldest society was the Anjuman-i-Punjab (established 1865), a mention of which has already been made in connection with the Punjab University. There were also societies having a special religious or national characteristic, *e.g.*, the Indian Association, the Arya Samaj, or the Anjuman-i-Islamia. Several of the more important societies published their own journals, while others were more or less represented by particular papers. The number of the various societies was thirty in the same year.

7

The Indian Education Commission 1882-83.

The limitations of time and space do not admit of our considering in this work the causes which led to the appointment of the Indian Educational Commission in February, 1882. Nor is it possible for us to note its detailed recommendations about the various aspects and branches of education investigated by it. Keeping in view the fact that the period treated of in this book closed about a year after the labours of the Commission ended, mention will be made of only those recommendations, action on which was called for in the Punjab as well as other Provinces, and any action taken or in contemplation by the close of 1884 will also be noticed.

The enquiries of the Commission embraced the working of all branches of the Indian educational system (excluding that in vogue in Burma) : primary, secondary, and collegiate, and female education, and the education of special classes and sections. Indian Universities and technical or special education were, however, not included so that the task before the Commission might not be unduly extended. The subject of the education of Europeans and Anglo-Indian had also been lately considered by the Bengal Committee appointed by the Government of

India and was, therefore, excluded from the terms of reference which guided the enquiries of the Commission.

The enquiry conducted by the Commission pertained particularly to the manner in which effect had been given to the principles of the despatch of 1854 and it was the duty of the Commission to suggest measures for further carrying out the policy laid down in it. An examination and a criticism of the basic structure outlined in that Despatch did not fall within the purview of the Commission which consequently proposed no drastic changes or departure, and the result of its labours was "a renewed enforcement and a further extension of the educational principles and policy prescribed in 1854."[1]

The Education Commission assembled at Calcutta in February 1882. Regarding education in the Punjab, it examined fifty three witnesses, inculding representatives of Literary Societies. Several statement were also received from persons interested in education. The Commission dissolved on the 16th of March, 1883, and its report was forwarded to the Goverument of India on 9th October, 1883.

The Chief recommendations of the Commission may now be summarised. Indigenous schools so far as these could be made to serve the purpose of secular education were to be recognised and encouraged and Municipal and Local Boards were to establish fresh schools of their own only where the preferable alternative of aiding suitable indigenous schools could not be adopted. Primary Education was to be regarded as the instruction of the masses through the varnaculars in subjects likely to fit them for their position in life and was

[1] Memorandum on some of the results of Indian Administration, 1911, Page 41.

not necessarily to be regarded ,as a portion of instruction leading up to the University. Practical subjects, such as native methods of arithmetic, accounts, and mensuration, the elements of natural and physical science, and their application to agriculture, health, and the industries, were, therefore, to be included in the scheme of studies for Primary Schools. Increased efforts were also to be made in favour of the extension of Primary Education and the cardinal principle was laid down that primary education was that part of the educational system, which possessed an exclusive claim on local funds set apart for education and a large claim on provincial revenues. As regards Secondary Educatian, it was distinctly declared that it was ordinarily expedient, on the part of the State, to provide the mean of secondary education only where adequate local co-operation was forth-coming. Secondary English Schools were, therefore, to be in furture established by the state on the footing of the grant-in-aid system. The establishment of secondary schools by Indian gentlemen would, it was believed, also lead to freedom and variety of education essential in any sound and complete educational sytem. Secondary Education was also to be rendered more practical by providing for a bifurcation of studies in the upper classes of high schools. Female Education was to be encouraged ; the standard of instruction was to be simpler than that for boys; additional normal schools on classes were to be established, Zenana teaching arranged by missionary societies was to be aided ; and above all, female inspecting agency was to be regarded an essential to the full development of female education. The system of scholarships was to be revised so as to make them open to all students without restriction and scholarships where henceforth to be distinct rewards for merit tested and proved by competitives examinations. Another recommondation concerned tuition fees which were to be raised gradually and cautiously. Conferences of officers of the Education Department and of such officers with managers of aided and unaided schools were to be held for the discussion of questions affecting education. Lastly, the strength of inspecting agency was to be increased and the remuneration of subordinate inspecting officers reconsidered with due regard to their enhanced duties and responsibilities.

There were also recommendaions concerning the moral training and physical development of scholars and the education of special clasess—Indian Chiefs, Mohammadans, and the depressed classes.

The narrative of the action taken or proposed to be taken in the Punjab upon these recommendations need not detain us long. It may be said at once that these received careful consideration at the hands of the Punjab Government and measures were soon adopted to give effect to them. A complete census of indigenous Schools existing in the Province was taken in 1882-83 and rewards were now distributed among those schools where useful secular instruction was being imparted. Information regarding the private Schools other than indigenous Schools was also obtained in 1884-85.

As regards Primary Education, assignments were made, from the year 1883-84, from Provincial revenues to aid Local Boards in the establishment of new Primary Schools and 136 new Schools had been opened by the close of the next financial year. The introduction of a village standard for theses schools was also in contemplation. A lady was appointed in 1883-84 for the inspection of the Indian girls' schools, though the appointment was at present only a temporary one. The system of High Schools Scholarships was, as described in the concluding section of the last chapter, completely revised in 1 83-84, and next year Local Bodies were also invited to declare a certain number of their Middle School Scholarships, calculated at the rate of one for every 150 scholars in the Primary stage, open to all residents of the district and tenable under certain fixed conditions which were uniform throught the province. Enhanced rate of tuition-fees for Colleges was introduced in 1883-84 and a similar scale for schools was introduced next year. The increase in fees was 16 per cent., while scholars had increased only by 6 percent. Fees for English instruction were now separated from those for Vernacular instruction and payment of fees by the sons of wealthy traders and rent-receiving landlords was enforced. For the improvement of the inspecting staff, a scheme was under consideration whereby the number of Assistant-Inspectors was to be raised to seven and every district, except Simla and Kohat, was to be provided with a District Inspector. Lastly, Conferences of Managers of aided Schools and Departemental Officers were also to be held every year in May. The measures, about the education of Indian Chiefs have already been described and attention was been directed to the education of Mohammadans and of the depressed classes.

CONCLUSION.

The educational system introduced in India in accordance with the principles contained in the despatch of 1854 was designed to fulfil a real demand on the part of certain classes which had, prior to the British rule, ever formed the administrative body of India. The measures adopted in the Punjab to give effect to the recommendations of the despatch have beeh described in the foregoing pages. It must be admitted that the introduction of a uniform system all over India was in the long run destined to produce a consciousness of a sense of unity among the people, and thus eventually lead to the dawning of a spirit of nationality among the various peoples inhabiting the vast sub-continent of India.

Momentous results such as these had, however, not yet appeared. The achievement of the period under consideration was that a standard to be aimed at for mass as well as higher education had been set and a beginning in the attainment of that standard had been made to some extent. The incorporation of the Punjab University in 1882 had assured due attention also to ancient learning and oriental culture in the province.

That these were no mean gains it may at once be conceded. How much yet remained to be done may, however, be judged from the state of instruction in Primary Schools in 1883-84. It was estimated that, of 14,21,989 boys between five and ten years who ought to have been at Primary Schools, only 196,901 boys, or one in 13·3 were attending such schools in the Province. This means that, although the education imparted at these schools was sound and real, not much had yet been achieved in the direction of that crying need of modern times, the spread of literacy among the masses.

The causes are not far to seek. The circumstances which necessitated the replacement of indigenous Schools by Schools on the new system were mentioned in an earlier chapter. But this policy of replacement meant in other words that, instead of any real extention of education among the masses, pupils formerly reading in indigenous Schools were now mainly transferred to the new schools established since 1856. It was therefore, the quality of instruction which had improved, while the quantity in terms of scholars under instruction remained practically unchanged.

Another cause of the infinitesimality of the growth of primary education lay in the celebrated Filtration Theory which so largely swayed the educational system in Bentinck's time. The theory had indeed been discarded by the authors of the despatch of 1854,[1] but that some effects of it still lingered may be gathered from a subsequent Despatch of the Court of Directors.[2] The eagerness of the upper classes for English education which would fit them for posts under the Government also worked in the same direction. The result was that sufficient funds were not devoted to primary education by Government ; indeed, the expenditure for that education was entirely met from local sources, and the contribution from Provincial revenues if made at all was very insignificant.

The prospect, was hopeful. In accordance with the recommendations of the Commission of 1882, strenous efforts of the State were now to be directed to the provision, extension, and improvement of Primary Education which would possess an almost exclusive claim on local funds set apart for education and a large claim on provincial revenues. Ths measures adopted in the Punjab to give effect to this new policy have been already described and an early progress in the extension of elementary education might now be hoped for.

---

[1] *Vide* Education Despatch of 1854, paragraph 41.
[2] Despatch 45, dated 18th April, 1855, paragraph 8.

Professional and technical education so essential for the industrial development of the country had not yet received the attention it deserved, but the fault probably lay more with the people, especially the Hindus, who did not realised the dignity of labour and were adverse from manual work as an occupation fit only for the Sudras.

The authors of the despatch of 1854 had not been disappointed in their hopes as regards the elevating influence of their system of education upon the character of the people. English or Western education had, in the words of Sir Richard Temple, "taught them truthfulness and honour both morally and intellectually."[1] But the effects of an education divorced from religion could not also escape observation. Youths educated at schools generally betrayed a spirit of irreverence for, and a tendency of destructive criticism of, their social and religious systems But the effects were not so glaring in the Punjab where one of the chief aims of the University was the encouragement of Oriental learning which was practically another name for the study of Hindu and Muslim cultures.

An educational movement must be a political movement in the sense that an educated man is able to place himself in the universe. The struggle for political rights must, however, remain primarily an economic one, and in as much as there was as yet no lack of employment for young men of fair education in the Punjab, "the general tone of the literature of the province, as shown in the registered publications......was moral and loyal ;[2]" and the energies of the people of the Punjab could be directed to the improvement of the moral, intellectual, and material well-being of the province.

The accompanying graphs[3] will perhaps show more clearly than anything else the progress of education during the period under discussion.

---

[1] Men and events of my time in India By Sir Richard Temple, page 430, quoted by Syed Mohmood in his English education in India.

[2] Punjab Administration Report, 1883-84,

[3] Appendix I.